THE "I" IN INDIAN

by BHAVNA BHATIA ROSZEL

THE "I" IN INDIAN

by BHAVNA BHATIA ROSZEL

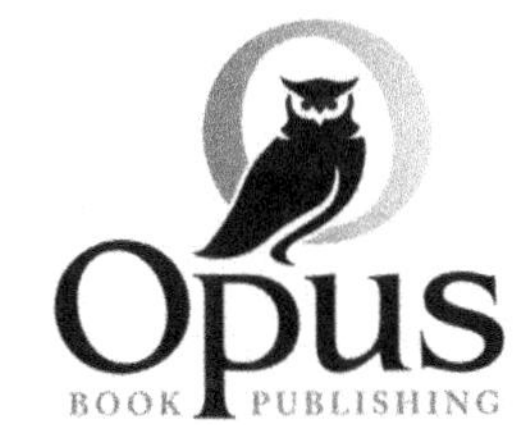

Opus Book Publishing

ISBN: 978-0-9898127-9-5

Unless otherwise indicated, all the characters in this book are fictitious. Any resemblance to actual persons, living or dead, is purely coincidental.

Front cover and book design by Opus Book Publishing

Printed by Opus Book Publishing in the United States of America

First printing 2025

PUBLISHER

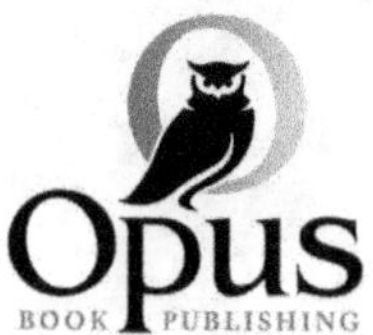

880 Harrsion St. SE
Leesburg, VA 20175
Opusbookpublishing.com

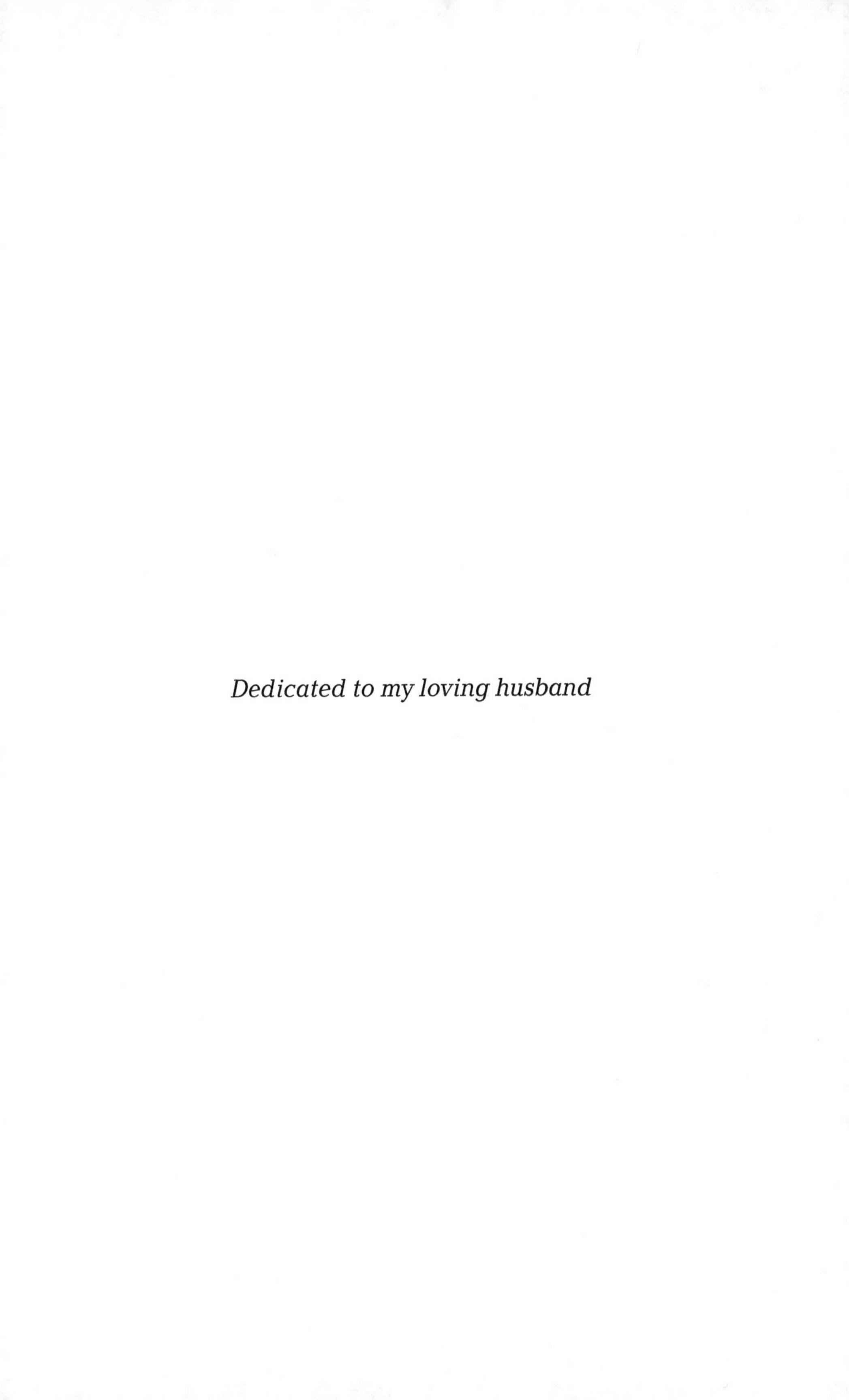

Dedicated to my loving husband

CHAPTER 1

LIFE'S PREFACE

"Here goes nothing," I mutter under my breath, tossing back a swig of my vodka soda in the parking lot of a dimly lit Mexican restaurant. Ten minutes late and already dreading what's inside, I know this is probably not the best way to start a date, but here we are. Date number... honestly, I've lost count. Let's call it 100. Or maybe 1,000. It's a blur of fails.

I pull down the rearview mirror for one last look. I run my fingers through my hair, which can never quite decide if it is curly or wavy. My eyeliner has the perfect thin wing, shaping my brown eyes. I take another sip of my drink while staring at myself. Vodka soda in the parking lot? Classy. But after a year of disappointments, you learn to take the edge off when and where you can. It is so exhausting to swipe through endless profiles, hold semi-decent conversations, and then realize—on the date—that the guy either photoshopped his entire face or is only interested in finding someone to "Netflix and chill."

At first, I thought ambition was the key—a guy with dreams, drive, and a plan for his life. But those men? Too busy chasing said dreams to actually text you back or, you know, show up emotionally.

So, I shifted gears—focused on guys who seemed attentive. Spoiler alert: Attention quickly morphed into "Aria...why didn't you text me back within 10 minutes?"

Then, there were the gym-obsessed with their selfies, the "look at my passport stamps" braggarts, the ones hunting for Stepford wives, and the ones so unsure of themselves they couldn't lead conversations, let alone relationships.

And then, there was the cultural challenge. For years, I stayed within my lane, using Indian-only dating apps like DilMil and Shaadi.com, assuming that someone from a similar background would be the easiest match. But the reality? Far from it.

My first date told me he expected his future wife to move in with his parents and cater to them. I haven't lived with my own parents for a decade; there was no way I was about to sign up for a joint family household.

The "I" in Indian

After that, I narrowed my search to Indian men who had been in the US for at least a decade. Surely, they'd be more assimilated. But the next guy I met said he'd prefer I didn't work and just stay home to raise kids. As a successful marketing director, that wasn't going to fly.

And the final straw? A guy who was thrilled I drank, calling me "so cool," only to follow up with, "But you know, you wouldn't be able to drink in front of my family. They wouldn't be on board with that."

I was defeated. Even if a guy had been in the States for years, it didn't mean his mentality—or his family's—had evolved.

So, I surrendered. I would stop filtering by race, by culture, by preconceived ideas of what my future husband should look like. I told myself it was just an experiment—just to see if there was a better alignment elsewhere. That's when I came across his profile.

Leo Roselli.

For starters, he's fully clothed in every photo, so that's already a win. He looks polished but not pretentious. Italian, I think, at least based on his name and dark features. There are pictures with friends, a family barbecue, a goofy shot where he's mid-laugh, with dimples that are hard to ignore. And then there's his answer to the profile prompt. "What are you looking for?" People usually answer with something painfully

vague like "Something casual" or "Something serious."
But his? "Someone who can make a great quesadilla."

I laughed. Out loud.

And it wasn't just the quirkiness. He seemed
self-aware, funny without trying too hard, and real. A
unicorn in the world of dating apps. So, I swiped right.
And here we are.

The rain outside matches my mood—slick,
unpredictable, and a little heavy. A rainy spring evening
in Virginia. He could have canceled, which plenty
of guys have done last minute—ghosted me with no
explanation. But he didn't. He's been doing everything
right so far. He asked me out (initiative, check), picked
an actual restaurant (effort, check), and even made a
reservation (follow-through, triple check). He texted to
confirm the plans earlier and kept me updated about his
arrival. If there were a Dating App Olympics, he'd be in
the running for gold.

And yet, here I am—sitting in my car—
procrastinating like it's a work deadline.

Why am I doing this? Why am I putting myself
through this carousel of awkward firsts and polite
goodbyes?

I blame Bollywood.

Growing up, I watched far too many movies about
the kind of love that defies logic, distance, and angry,

                                    The "I" in Indian

disapproving fathers. Men in those films would climb mountains, battle family feuds, and convert religions to prove their love. And, of course, I was hooked. Who wouldn't be? Those stories carved their way into my brain like a song you can't forget, teaching me that real love was worth fighting for.

But my parents' reality? Quite the opposite of a Bollywood movie. Following a traditional arranged marriage, they were decently happy, but nothing like what was sold in those films. No grand gestures. No passionate serenades in the rain. Just a quiet, pragmatic companionship that works. And yet, despite seeing that reality up close, I still hold fast to the fantasy.

So, yes, my life looks nothing like a Bollywood movie, either. But a small, stubborn part of me can't let go of "The Dream." Somewhere out there is my person. The one who will fight for me, who will see every messy, complicated piece of who I am and love me anyway.

And maybe, just maybe, he'll even be funny.

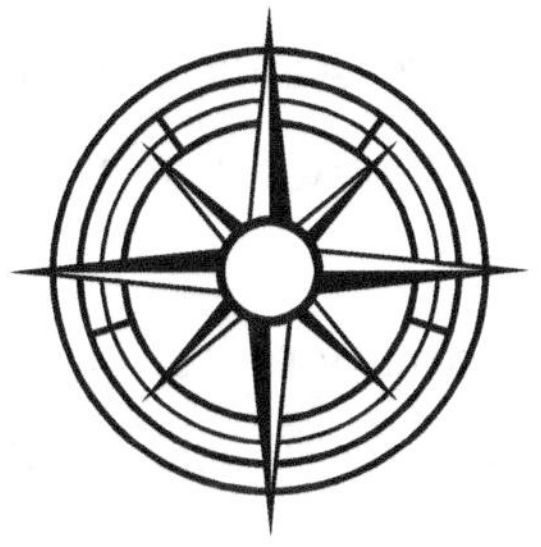

CHAPTER 2

SETTING SAIL

Bro, I don't hate Virginia. I mean, I grew up here. But, as soon as I was done with high school, I booked. I chased the ocean breeze straight to Hilton Head. There, my life was all about the water—first boat restoration then first mate on a ship and finally captain. It was unpredictable, lively, full of adventure—everything I thought I wanted. But, man, as much as I dug the chaos, I knew it wasn't a place to, you know, "adult."

So, with 30 on the horizon and a not-so-subtle nudge from my parents, I came back to Virginia three years ago. There's something to be said about the area—the country roads, the bustling capital, the mountains, and the beaches. It feels like, I don't know, a buffet of everything life has to offer. Middletown is in horse country—"picturesque" according to realtors, with sprawling estates and more wineries (and breweries) than you can count. I understand why my parents wanted to raise me here.

But...damn, the dating pool here is about as exciting as waiting for barnacles to grow. Occasionally, a bachelorette party might blow through town, or I'll flirt with someone new at the local pub. Or I'll meet someone who's in town for a horse show. But they are all gone by the end of the weekend. The pool for having a meaningful relationship around these parts is emptier than a marina on a Monday.

My friends at work, always full of unsolicited advice, insisted that I download a dating app. In the teachers' lounge: "It's the only way to meet someone outside this bubble." And even in the parking lot: "Dude, you've got to get out of bumblefuck if you want to meet someone!"

I resisted for a while, thinking dating apps were for guys who couldn't hack it in the real world. But after a very dull Friday night, I gave in. Hinge, here we go.

Setting up a profile was painful. Like...do I lead with the fact that I once ate an entire block of cheddar in one sitting? Or that I cried during a Subaru commercial? Tough choice, that. How do I make myself stand out? "Loves long walks on the beach and sunsets"? PL-eeze. I might as well throw in that I want a puppy and a white picket fence. And maybe a pet turtle named Steve. You know, to really show I've got layers.

The prompts didn't help either. "What are you looking

                                    The "I" in Indian

for?" Soulmate? Adventure buddy? Someone who'll put up with my love of terrible dad jokes. It all felt so stupid.

So, instead of overthinking it, I went with the one thing I knew to be true: I fucking love cheese. If I could eat one thing for the rest of my life, it would be cheese. That's what I wrote: *Looking for someone who can make a great quesadilla.*

A few days later, I got a message: *I bet I can make the best quesadilla you've ever had.*

Bold, confident, and funny. I liked her already. Then, I checked out her profile, and my jaw practically hit the floor.

Aria Kapoor. She was stunning. Picture after picture of this gorgeous Indian woman with a smile so captivating I couldn't look away. Her big brown eyes, her long hair, her skin—it all felt unreal. She lived more than 30 miles away, so it's no wonder I had never seen her in Middletown. Could she be a catfish? Maybe. But I was determined to find out—one way or another.

I had never dated a non-white woman before. Not because I was opposed to it—just because I grew up in Bumblefuck, Virginia, where diversity was lacking, to say the least. The few Indian kids at school were either in my brother's grade or kept to their own circle. South Carolina was no different. The majority of people there were white—and old.

In my defense, I am not some ignoramus. My parents had not raised me that way. They treated everyone the same—no matter where they came from or what they looked like. My mom, especially, had this way of making everyone feel like they belonged, like they were family. And let's be real: How could any dude resist beautiful olive skin and long, shiny hair? Certainly, not me. I set up a date immediately.

The restaurant was packed and buzzing like you can only get outside Middletown. Aurburn was a suburb just a half-hour outside DC (an hour or more during rush hour), but light-years from my quiet, stuffy hometown.

I pick a booth by the window, the perfect spot to take in the energy of the place. Spanish music pulses through the space. Just being here feels like a refreshing change from Middletown's sleepy calm.

I tell myself again to keep my expectations low. Maybe she shows up; maybe she doesn't. Maybe she looks like her pictures; maybe she doesn't. I am going to treat this like a chance to get out of my comfort zone, nothing more.

But when the door swings open and the waitress points her in my direction, every ounce of my cool flies out the window.

She is breathtaking. Her long, shiny black hair falls perfectly over her shoulders, and her fitted maxi skirt with purple flowers hugs her in all the right ways. She has an effortless confidence, flashing the waitress a kind smile before making her way toward me.

I stand up and extend my hand to introduce myself. But she goes straight in for a hug. It catches me off-guard, but I am not complaining. She fits perfectly against me, and I can't help but notice how tiny she is. My hand briefly lands on the small of her back. Before I know it, my eyes dart lower.

Yep, I am in trouble.

We pull apart, and I immediately feel like I need to say something, anything, to keep from looking like an idiot.

"I brought avocados..." The words tumble out before I can stop them.

Her brow furrows, and she looks around, clearly confused. "Were they running low in the kitchen? Well, aren't you helpful!" she teases, carrying on like I haven't just embarrassed myself in the first five seconds of our meeting. I want to crawl under the table and become one with the guacamole.

Thankfully, the waitress appears to take our drink orders, giving me a moment to recover. A few sips of margarita later, and I am back on my game.

During the next few hours, I can't stop asking her questions. I want to know everything—about her job as a marketing director for a national furniture magazine, about her younger sister with whom she is very close, about the college dance team she used to belong to. I love that she hopes to ride the glacier express in Switzerland one day.

The more she talks, the more I find myself captivated—not just by her beauty but by her sharp wit and the way her whole face lights up when she speaks.

"So, Leo, what took you to South Carolina?" she asks. I am not typically one to share my story easily, but, around her, I feel differently—like I want her to know me.

"Well, I grew up in the middle of nowhere. It would take 20 minutes just to drive to the nearest gas station. I wanted to experience living somewhere where I could walk to restaurants and stores. I liked it down there, but the people were transient, and the work didn't feel meaningful. So, I am back here in the middle of nowhere. But this time it feels different."

"Well, I am glad you came back," she says, smiling shyly. "You're a teacher now, right?" she asks. Okay, she must have Googled me.

"Yeah. I work at a private school that has students from 1st through 8th grade. I like seeing them grow up."

Her smile lights her soft eyes. She says, "That's really beautiful."

Becoming a teacher was quite a change for me. It is hard, so it is an accomplishment I am proud of. In the past, this profession had worked against me on dates. Some girls would hear "teacher" and automatically assume I'm broke. Aria's quiet admiration and simple acceptance gives me a warm thump in my chest I didn't expect.

She has this natural charisma, the kind that pulls you in and makes you want to stay. The entire evening passes with easy conversation and a lot of laughs. And when she suggests a "rapid-fire round" to test my honesty, I am game.

"What are you looking for?" she asks.

"Someone to marry," I say, not even flinching.

"Do you believe in monogamy?"

"Yes."

"Do you want kids?"

"Yes. Preferably the kind that think dad jokes are cool."

"Do you believe in God?"

"On holidays, mostly. And anytime the Washington Commanders win, which is rare."

"Are you an American citizen?"

I pause, caught off-guard by the question That was a first. I cautiously say, "Yes."

She stares at me, her dark eyes narrowing—like she is trying to read my soul. It is both intimidating and adorable. After a moment, she smiles—a real, genuine smile—and I feel like I have passed some kind of test and secured another date.

By the time we leave, the restaurant staff is practically shoving us out the door. It has been 4 hours, but it feels like no time has passed at all. As we walk to her car, a light drizzle starts to fall. I hold an umbrella over her, walking slower than necessary—just to make the moment last.

When we reach her car, she turns to say goodbye, and I know I can't let the night end without kissing her. So, I lean in. To my relief, she leans in, too. Her lips are soft and sweet, tasting faintly of strawberry margaritas.

As she drives away, I stand there, soaked and grinning like an idiot.

I've got to thank my fellow teachers at school tomorrow.

CHAPTER 3

KAPOORIAN LUNCH

Sunday lunches were a standard in the Kapoor household, but this Sunday is extra special because my little sister, Saira, is going to be joining us. She recently moved close to complete her medical residency. I'm so excited to be splitting the burden of these lunches with her. It's also been weeks since we've had a proper chat about how things have been progressing with Leo.

The aroma of cumin, coriander, and turmeric filled the air, wrapping the dining room in a fragrant warmth that felt like home. My parents' house had always smelled this way, like a never-ending stream of curries simmering on the stove. The table was set meticulously (as always): a spread of dal, bhindi masala, steaming basmati rice, and stacks of perfectly round rotis resting under a clean kitchen towel.

As we sat down, Saira and I exchanged glances. Despite the four years between us, we had grown up thicker than thieves, navigating these awkward lunches together. We'd perfected the art of silent communication during years of sharing a room. Just one flick of her eyebrow, and I already knew what she was thinking: Buckle up, here comes the Spanish Inquisition. With her now knowing where she would be doing her residency as an internal medicine doctor, we just knew that the conversation of today's lunch would revolve around that.

My mother, Shama Kapoor, sat at the circular wooden table, her posture impeccable as always. Her short black hair perfectly framed her chin. She had been raised under the rigid discipline of her father, a brigadier general in the Indian army. Her entire life had been structured, bound by etiquette, rules, and the constant pressure to be proper. And she is exactly that—a composed, controlled woman who embodies grace and obedience.

She had married my father, Vishal Kapoor, through an arrangement. He was the son of a fellow army man. Were they in love? I am not sure. But they had done everything by the book.

They got married as soon as they completed college, moved to the US to build up businesses that would send money back home, and provided us with a comfortable life. No scandals of their own, no public drama, and great reputations in the community. They are the epitome of what you're supposed to do.

Saira and I both knew how this lunch would go before it even started. The script never changed.

"Saira, beta," my dad starts, scooping rice onto his plate, "we are so happy you will be staying close to home for your residency. You know your mother is already planning how she will bring you home-cooked meals every week."

"And we can drop by to see you whenever we want," my mom adds with a satisfied smile, as if this was the best news she had ever delivered.

Saira forces a smile. "Yeah... that sounds great," she says, her tone flat. I notice how her fingers tighten around her fork.

My dad, oblivious to her lack of enthusiasm, continues. "And, while you're in residency, you should keep your eyes open. There will be plenty of nice Indian doctors there. It's a good time to start thinking about settling down."

Saira, still smiling, gives a noncommittal shrug and shoves a bite of rice into her mouth, expertly dodging the topic.

I couldn't help myself. "Does he have to be an Indian doctor? What about an Indian nurse? Or an Indian janitor?" I quip, raising an eyebrow. I am mostly joking, but I already know it won't go over well.

The table falls silent. My mother shoots me a death glare so sharp, I feel it in my bones. Saira kicks me under the table. I wince and drop the conversation.

The air shifts, thick with unspoken tension. That is the thing about lunches in this house. So much of what could be said is never said. Certain topics are simply off-limits, ignored—buried under pleasantries and the pretense of normalcy.

To break the awkward silence, my mom clears her throat. "Some mail came for you this week, Aria." She hands me an envelope, thick and ornate, with gold, embossed lettering.

Saira leans over to read it. "Finally!"

I rip the envelope open, my heart skipping as I pull out an extravagant wedding invitation. The intricate Indian designs, the shimmering gold foil, the overwhelming grandness of it. It is unmistakable.

"Veera's wedding invitation is here!" Saira and I squeal in unison.

We had been expecting it. But still, seeing it in person makes it all the more exciting. Veera Singh, my best friend, and used-to-be man-hater, is really doing it. She is getting married. Even more shocking? She is marrying an Indian man. Oh, how far we have come.

My father, who has been watching quietly, finally speaks up. "Isn't Veera the friend with all the tattoos? The one who is estranged from her family?"

I clench my jaw. I want to defend Veera, to remind him that she is the most fiercely loyal person I know, that her tattoos don't define her, and that there is a good reason she isn't speaking to her family. But I don't. What would be the point? Instead, I just shrug and look back down at the invitation.

We take the invitation upstairs to our old bedroom (now a guest room), which is still preserved with the same pink-and-purple quilted covers we grew up with. Saira plops down and asks, "I wonder if her parents are coming to the wedding?"

I shrug again. "I'll get the full scoop at the end of the month. Vegas tradition," I say with a grin.

Saira smirks. "Ah, yes, the annual pilgrimage to the land of bad decisions and overpriced cocktails."

"Hey, it's a decade-strong tradition," I shoot back. " I can't wait to get all the deets about her wedding."

Sitting cross-legged on my childhood bed, I turn to Saira. "Okay, so what was that at lunch? You don't seem thrilled about staying close to home."

Saira sighs, falling back against the pillows. "It's just... I spent the past several years away at med school, completely free to do what I wanted. It was so easy to keep my life separate from our parents'. The parties, the drinking, the dating... They never knew about any of it. And now?" She exhales sharply. "Now, I have to be so much more careful."

I frown. "Why don't you just tell them you want space? That you're an adult and you need your privacy?"

Saira turns her head to look at me, raising an eyebrow. "Oh? And when are you going to tell them about your white boy?"

I scowl. "Touché."

She grins. "See? It's not just me. We both have things we're not ready to share."

She wasn't wrong. I know she is teasing, but, somewhere deep inside, I also know the truth: I am the rebel of the family. Shama and Vishal Kapoor followed tradition. They married who their parents wanted them to, had children, worked hard and aimed to instill the same values in their children that were instilled in them. And here I am, a perfect example of what not to do—heading off to Las Vegas with my fellow rebellious best friend and keeping secrets my parents could never understand.

The "I" in Indian

I guess we are both making choices to preserve the peace. Maybe one day, we'll be ready to be completely open. But today is not that day. Instead, we exchange a silent understanding. For now, our secrets are safe.

As I tuck the invitation back into its envelope, Saira gives me a look. "So, tell me more about Leo. What's he like?"

I hesitate, then allow a small smile. "Well, he's a teacher, which I absolutely love."

Saira raises an eyebrow. "A teacher?"

"Yeah. He wants to live a life that feels meaningful to him and help shape the future of kids' lives. It's inspiring really. Don't get me wrong. I am totally passionate about my career, but I am helping companies make more money, not changing the world."

Saira, not allowing me to self-deprecate, says teasingly, "You are still making a difference. So many people have bought beautiful things for their home because of the ads you put in your magazine!"

I roll my eyes and carry on. "I mean, it's not like teachers are paid well, but they should be, don't you think? I admire him for following his passion. Teachers shape the future, but they just aren't respected as much as, say, doctors."

Saira doesn't say anything. Of course, she can't. She is about to enter a profession that commands respect precisely because of its prestige and pay. Admitting I am right would mean admitting the whole system is flawed.

Instead, she smirks. "Are you bringing him to the wedding?"

I freeze for a second before recovering. "Of course not. No one knows about Leo, and I plan to keep it that way."

Saira smirks but doesn't press the issue. She simply tucks the invitation under her pillow. "My lips are sealed."

CHAPTER 4

THE COACH'S GIRL

The cool metal of the bleachers presses against my
legs as I sit on the sidelines of the lacrosse field, trying to
keep my nerves in check. The Mill School Dragons are
about to storm the field for their big match against the
Wakefield Warriors. Even though I know nothing about
lacrosse, I can't help but feel a little giddy. Leo invited
me here, to his turf, to see him in action.

He's told me a hundred times how much he loves
coaching—how it's one of the most rewarding parts
of his job. But hearing about it and witnessing it are
two very different things. This feels significant—like a
glimpse into his world, one that I've only heard about in
passing conversations over drinks or late-night phone
calls, which have become a daily thing.

The school itself is ridiculous. The Mill School isn't

just a school; it's a campus—a private-school-meets-Ivy-League hybrid. The cobblestone pathways, the perfectly manicured lawns, the picturesque schoolhouses straight off a movie set. Even the Blue Ridge Mountains in the background look like they've been positioned for maximum Instagramability. I mean, this place was clearly designed to churn out future senators, tech moguls, or whatever impressive titles rich kids aspire to these days.

It's a stark contrast to my own work view. My view is a laptop with an attached double screen. My days are filled with a myriad of editorial, marketing, and graphic design meetings. My office is in my townhome, where my most impressive view is the back of someone else's home. I stare at these idyllic surroundings, and suddenly, Leo's easy confidence—his lightness— makes sense. When you spend your days in a place like this— close to nature and in fresh air—it's bound to seep into you.

The Dragons finally charge onto the field, their energy electric as they jog a lap around the perimeter, soaking in the cheers from the crowd. And there he is. Leo. Jogging alongside the team with the same energy. He waves to the students and parents in the stands, his grin as humble as it is effortless. He's dressed in his "coach uniform"—blue athletic shorts, a crisp white t-shirt, and that green dragon-emblazoned hat. He looks good, too good, the kind of good that makes you lose track of time for a second.

And then his eyes find mine in the stands, and he winks.

A group of 13-year-old girls sitting in front of me burst into giggles, whispering excitedly and clearly wishing that wink had been for them. Honestly, I get it. If I were 13, I'd have a poster of him on my wall. Heck, I might get one now.

"Which one is yours?" a mom seated next to me asks. Her tone is warm, curious. I glance over at her, realizing that I probably stand out here among the sea of parents.

"Oh, I'm here for Coach Leo," I reply with a smile, gesturing toward him on the field.

Her eyes widen in surprise before her face softens into a knowing grin. "Coach Leo?" she says, nudging me playfully with her elbow. "He's a good one. All the kids adore him. My son, Trey, is right there, number 7. Leo is so patient with him, and it's helped him so much."

I can feel the warmth of her words spreading through me, leaving a glow that lingers. It's one thing to see Leo through my own eyes, but hearing how he's admired makes my heart swell. Sitting here in the stands, watching him coach, I feel a quiet pride.

It's strange, really. In the past few years, I have considered myself pretty independent, not needing a partner to feel validated—or maybe resigned to the idea that I may never find my person. But what I feel right now is different. It's not about me needing him; it's about me wanting him to know how much I see him. How much I appreciate the person he is, both on and off this field.

The Dragons gather in a huddle, and Leo crouches in the center, gesturing animatedly as he gives them a pep talk. I can't hear what he's saying, but I can see it on their faces. They're focused, nodding along, grinning at whatever joke he's slipped in. He's got them eating from the palm of his hand, and it's no wonder.

Sitting here, watching him in his element, I realize something. This isn't just a glimpse into his world; it's a glimpse into the kind of person he is—someone who inspires, someone who cares, someone who, even in the middle of a lacrosse game, can make you feel like you're exactly where you're meant to be.

CHAPTER 5
WINNING THE GAME

The game is tied. One minute to go. And Trey, Trey is on fire. The kid has talent—speed, agility, the kind of raw skill you just can't teach. But he's also an emotional tornado. He cries when he scores, cries when he doesn't, cries when someone else scores. I love his passion. But right now? Right now, I need him to channel it, not drown in it.

I pull him to the side, draping an arm over his narrow shoulders. His small frame leans into me, his wide eyes scanning my face for reassurance.

"Do you think I'm going to mess up, Coach?" he asks, his voice barely above a whisper.

I crouch down to his level, gripping his shoulders so he feels steady. "Trey, here's what I know," I say firmly. "You've worked your ass off. You've got the skills, the focus, and the fire. The rest? That's just noise. You've got this."

His eyes brighten, and a determined nod tells me he's ready. He jogs back onto the field, his head held high, and I feel that familiar mix of nerves and pride. This is what it's all about—seeing these kids rise to the occasion.

As I walk back to the sideline, I catch myself scanning the stands for Aria, again. I've done it a dozen times already today. When our eyes meet, she quickly glances away, pretending to focus on something else, but I know better. The thought makes me grin like an idiot.

Having her here changes things. It's one thing to talk about spending your life with someone, but it's another to have them step into it, to see them cheer you on. It pulls at something deep inside me, something I hadn't quite put a name to until now.

My parents, Maria and Tony Roselli, set the bar impossibly high. High school sweethearts who have now spent nearly 40 years together, still holding hands like teenagers. Whenever I ask them the secret, they always say the same thing: "You have to accept each other—for all the good, the bad, and the ugly."

For years, I've been looking for that—someone who would accept me, flaws and all, someone who wouldn't just be around for the easy parts but would show up for me through thick and thin. And, as I watch Aria in the stands, so

                                    The "I" in Indian

fully present, so genuinely excited for me, I start to wonder if this could be something real. It feels... big. Bigger than I expected.

The referee's whistle pulls me back to the game. Matty, one of our attackers, has the ball. He's darting down the field. His focus is sharp. But, the defenders are closing in fast. The clock ticks down: 10 seconds, 9, 8.... Matty glances around frantically and spots Trey, who's managed to shake his defender and position himself perfectly outside the goal.

Matty passes. Trey catches. One clean shot into the net, and the crowd explodes.

Trey's teammates swarm him, hoisting him into the air as the parents in the stands erupt. Watching the boys' pure, unfiltered joy fills me with pride. Moments like this remind me why I coach. It's not about the wins; it's about what the wins teach the kids. Teamwork. Resilience. Confidence. These are the lessons that will stick.

The opposing coach approaches. We exchange a firm handshake. My focus, though, is already drifting back to Aria. She's on her feet, clapping and shouting with a smile so bright it feels like it's just for me.

Growing up, my parents weren't around much for my games. They worked hard—overtime, double shifts, whatever it took to keep us afloat. I don't blame them, but I can't deny that I used to wish someone was there, watching, cheering, showing me they cared. Seeing Aria here, so fully present, fills a part of me I didn't even know was empty.

I wave her over, and she practically bounces down the bleachers to meet me.

"That was amazing!" she says, her excitement bubbling over. "You were amazing! Congratulations, Coach!"

Her energy is infectious, and I can't help but laugh. I want to tell her exactly how much it means to me that she's here, but instead, I lean into the moment.

"Let's get out of here," I say, unable to hide the grin tugging at my lips.

She tilts her head, confused. "Don't you want to celebrate with your team? The parents have been raving about you all afternoon. They probably want to talk to you, take pictures...."

I shake my head, cutting her off gently. "I don't coach for the spotlight. Besides, I can think of better ways to celebrate." I take her hand, lacing my fingers through hers, and start leading her toward the parking lot.

Her cheeks flush, but she doesn't pull away. "You're ridiculous," she mutters, but there's a hint of a smile playing on her lips.

As we walk, her hand snug in mine, I feel a quiet certainty settle in my chest. The game was a win, sure. But the real victory? It's right here beside me.

"So, what are you doing this weekend?" I ask casually, squeezing her hand.

     The "I" in Indian

Aria sighs dramatically. "Oh, I see. You are already trying to see me again, huh?" she says with mock sympathy. "I'm heading to Vegas with Veera. We have a wedding to plan, and let's be real. If I'm not there to keep her in check, she might decide to hire on a tiger to be ring bearer."

I quickly scan my memory to remember exactly who Veera is. Oh, yes. How could I forget that high-pitched voice when she animatedly told me about what she described as Aria's BFF-AE AE? I mean, really, WTF is that?

And what is it with girls and Vegas? They're always trying to run off to Vegas to be "free" without any accountability. I laugh but feel a twinge of something else— something, I don't know, "possessive?"

Suddenly, the thought of her being out there with other men gawking at her obvious beauty annoys me. Aria is special. She's the kind of woman you don't let slip through your fingers. And if I'm not careful, someone else is going to realize that before I do.

I better lock this girl down sooner rather than later.

CHAPTER 6

REALITY...FROM A CERTAIN POINT OF VIEW

Leo

Have you told them about me yet?

Aria

Now why would I do that?

Leo

Because I'm adorable?

Aria

Rolling my eyes 🙄

Leo

Our typical gathering for a family meal this week
had been shifted to accommodate the fact that I would
be in Vegas this weekend. My parents probably aren't
thrilled about this. But, at this point, they have given
up trying to stand between Veera and me. The scent of
spiced potatoes in a tangy curry fills the kitchen, and the
sound of hot puris sizzling in oil crackles in the air.

Saira, catching my grinning at my phone, kicks me
under the table and gives me big eyes, so that I don't get
caught.

I quickly put my phone away, but my grin remains
on my face. This wasn't really what I had in mind when
I had accepted Leo's invitation to a date. I thought I
would just take a break from looking for an acceptable
husband and go out casually with some random guy. I
never seriously considered that I might actually start
liking one—a lot.

I reach for a puri, carefully tear off a piece, and hope
that I am not giving myself away. My mother, sitting
across from me, eyes me like she is waiting for the right
moment to strike.

She sets a fresh puri on my plate. "Did you hear

The "I" in Indian

about Geet?" Her voice is casual, but I know better.

I pause mid-bite. Phew, at least it's not about Leo. "What about her?"

My father scoffs and shakes his head as he scoops up some curry with his roti. "Another proposal rejected. The boy was suitable—a surgeon—and from a well-to-do family. They had even had all the discussions around an arrangement—until he found out she is a divorced woman."

"Geet has really put herself in trouble," my mother adds. "She just had to go run off with that German man and get married without her parents' blessing. Two years later, he abandoned her. Kicked her out of his house like she is nothing. Now look at her—she's almost 40 and has no chance of having children. No suitable man will even give her a second look. Do you remember how she came back to us?"

I don't respond, but the memory is quite vivid. Geet, my once vibrant and outgoing cousin, returned home to India with nothing but shame. She became the whispered cautionary tale at every family gathering.

A familiar tightness wraps around my chest. "That's awful," I say, my appetite disappearing. "It was so long ago. Does she even want to get married again?"

My mother clicks her tongue. "Aria, you always have to stir the pot, don't you? Of course, Geet needs to get married again, and no one wants her. No one will even give her a chance. People still think this way, Aria. It's reality."

"But why?" I press. "He kicked her out. It sounds like she didn't have much of a choice. Why is it such a big deal?"

My father slams his spoon down onto the plate, the sound sharp and final. "Enough," he commands. "We are not discussing this."

I look over at Saira, hoping for support. But, she keeps her head down, focusing on her plate, not wanting to get involved. Deflated, I take another bite, letting the conversation die out as we finish our meal in silence.

Later that evening, I sit on my balcony with a glass of Cabernet in hand, enjoying the spring breeze. I recently had the long balcony painted a warm cedar color. I added a dark wicker sectional with cream-colored cushions. After visiting Leo's Middletown, I decided to hang string lights above and position some large Majesty Palms in every corner—to make the space feel more natur-esque. Tonight, it felt like a

The "I" in Indian

little sanctuary from my mother's harsh words: "This is reality. Divorced women have a hard time."

The truth is Geet isn't the only divorcee in the family. I, too, am divorced.

We never speak about it. No one ever brings it up—not for a long time now. In fact, I have buried that part of my past, shoved it so deep down that sometimes I am almost convinced myself it was never real.

But it was. And now, sitting alone with my thoughts, I can't escape it.

Looking through the French doors, I see an impeccable open floor townhome. The walls are painted a warm off-white, complementing the exposed wooden ceiling beams that add a touch of historic character.

At the center of the room sits a plush, oversized sectional in a neutral taupe. Woven and plaid throw pillows adorn the sofa with earthy tones of beige, sage green, and rust. A cozy knitted blanket drapes perfectly over one arm, inviting relaxation.

A weathered wooden coffee table with sturdy, turned legs takes center stage, topped with a decorative wooden tray holding a mix of candles in vintage glass holders, a small potted olive tree, and a stack of well-loved books. Beneath it, a large, vintage Persian rug in muted blues, creams, and terra cottas adds depth and warmth. It looks like a catalog ad. I guess being part of the home furnishings industry has its perks.

From so many vantage points, I am considered extremely successful. I have built a beautiful life for myself. I am educated, a homeowner, successful in my career, healthy, and a good person, if I may say so myself. And yet, in my parents' eyes—in society's eyes—none of it matters as much as the fact that my marriage ended.

I rarely bring up my divorce in the early phases of dating. To me, it's something that should come up naturally as you get to know each other, something you share in a moment of vulnerability. It's not something I think I should announce right away as some sort of disqualifier. But, if I am being honest, my mother isn't totally off-base. I went out with this one Indian guy a few times and felt it was the right time to tell him. Now, he didn't blatantly end things with me because I was divorced, but he conveniently got very busy once he knew. Eventually, he stopped calling altogether. I got the message.

I swirl my wine, my mind drifting to Leo. Would he care? Would he look at me differently if he knew?

A small seed of doubt creeps in. He never judged me for anything before, but this is different. This is something I have seen ruin women's lives. What if it ruins mine?

I exhale, leaning back against the cushion, trying to shake the thought. But deep down, I know. This fear isn't going anywhere. Sooner or later, I would have to face it.

But for now: Vegas.

CHAPTER 7

A DIFFERENT POINT OF VIEW

The moment I spot Veera at the airport, my heart lifts. It's been an entire year since we've seen each other in person. But, thanks to FaceTime, we haven't missed a beat. She looks exactly the same—round face, wild hair, and thick, stylish glasses—utterly confident. I pick up my pace, dragging my carry-on behind me, as she throws her arms open.

"There she is!" she exclaims, pulling me into a tight hug. "Missed your face, A!"

"Missed you more, V," I reply, squeezing her back. Seeing her again is like a shot of happiness straight to my veins. No matter how much time passes, Veera and I always pick up right where we left off. We've been through too much together not to.

"Here, let me take your bag," she slings my backpack over her shoulder and links her arm with mine. "I made a playlist of our favorite Bollywood songs to hear on the way to the hotel," she grins. I can already tell this is going to be an amazing trip.

We quickly make our way to the Bellagio, settling into our usual room—just like we have done for the past 10 years. This trip is our annual escape, our tradition—a break from reality when we reconnect and remind ourselves of how far we have come. Sharing a room always brings us back to our 20s, when we lived together, navigating heartbreaks, family struggles, career choices, and the never-ending quest for self-acceptance. It's comforting, familiar—like slipping into an old, favorite sweater.

After freshening up, we head down to the bar, where Veera orders me a vodka soda with lime without even asking. "Some things never change," she teases, sliding the glass over.

The Bellagio water show is in full force behind us as we settle onto the open terrace, the crisp and dry West Coast air perfect, the city alive with reckless energy.

I take a sip of my drink and grin. " I still can't believe you're actually getting married."

Veera laughs, shaking her head. "I know, right?

                        The "I" in Indian

Who would've thought the Anti-Indian-Man Enthusiast would be here, engaged to one?"

I laugh, nodding along, "Okay, so last we spoke, you were deciding if you wanted to get henna done the night before or not. What did you decide?"

Right then, we are interrupted by a young girl who approached, waving and hollering excitedly to see Veera. Veera stood up, surprised but welcoming. "Hey there, what a surprise! What are you doing here in Vegas?" Veera asks as she gives the woman a hug. "I'm here on a bachelorette! What are you doing here? Small world, huh?" the woman replies. Veera looks back at me, realizing I am puzzled. "Aria, this is Sapna. We met at a music festival last year in California. Actually, it's the same music festival where Krish and I met!"

I stand up to shake her hand, "Hi, Sapna, nice to meet you." She smiles warmly and asks, "I remember you and Krish from that weekend. So, you guys are still an item, huh?" she asks playfully.

"Actually," Veera continues, putting her ring finger up for display, "we're getting married in 3 months!"

Sapna grabs her hand, and her eyes almost pop out of her face. "Wow, this is so beautiful. Congratulations! Where is the wedding? Is this your bachelorette as well?"

Veera laughs. "This is my annual getaway with

my bestie, Aria. As far as the wedding goes, it's a small ceremony, taking place at a Hindu temple in New Jersey—the new one that went viral for its all-marble floors. No fuss, just a handful of people, Including some friends and Krish's sister. We're keeping it simple."

Sapna smiles, "Simple...that's not how I imagined you'd get married."

Veera gives me a glance that only I can read. Shows how well Sapna knows her. Veera exchanges a few more pleasantries and then we say our goodbyes, getting back to our intimate time.

Once it's just us again, I shake my head in disbelief. "I mean, forget the wedding details. I'm still processing you settling down. You, of all people, putting faith in someone for the long haul?"

· "Shit. After what happened to you, I was almost scared off marriage for life," she laughs. "But, on a serious note, how many nights did we spend talking, soul-searching, healing, forgiving?" She gives me a pointed look. "You know as well as I do. This did **not** come easily."

I nod, remembering those nights vividly. The long talks, the emotional wreckage we sorted through together.

"Speaking of healing," Veera adds, her tone shifting. "Before you even ask...No, my parents are absolutely not

                          The "I" in Indian

coming to my wedding."

I blink, surprised. "Wait. What?"

She leans back in her chair, exhaling slowly. "It's a miracle I managed to be with an Indian guy after everything I saw growing up. The last thing I need is a reminder of them on my wedding day."

I struggle to wrap my head around it. "Not inviting either of your parents? That's... bold. I don't think I could ever do that."

Veera studies me for a second before speaking. "Think about it, Aria. What kind of relationship do we Indian girls really have with our parents? With our fathers, we don't talk about anything real. We're raised to respect them but not to know them. And they don't really know us, either."

I think of my father's spoon slamming down just days before, the unspoken rules at our table, the surface-level conversations that never go beyond work, duty, expectations.

"It's not just fathers, though," Veera continues. "Mothers are their own kind of complication. They don't prepare us for life; they prepare us for marriage. That used to be their sole purpose—being a wife. Back in their time, when women got married through arrangements, they were sometimes like business transactions. The daughters were sent away with their

dowries to live with their husbands and in-laws—
sometimes never seeing their own families again.

"Mothers are just so obsessed with making sure we
fulfill our purpose, too. Naturally, the relationship stays
surface level forever. They don't ask about our dreams,
our happiness, our ambitions, because none of that
matters. All that matters is whether we will make good
wives."

I exhale, feeling a familiar tightness in my chest.
"And sons?" I add, "They never had to deal with any of
that."

Veera lets out a dry laugh. "Of course not. Sons are
golden children. Parents invest in them because they
are the ones who stay. They aren't sent away. They bring
their wives home to take care of the parents. Meanwhile,
we are raised to leave. To serve someone else's family.
No wonder they never bother getting close to us."

I stare into my drink, the ice clinking as I swirl it
around. "And when things go wrong, it's always the
woman who bears the shame. If she's divorced, she's
damaged goods. Doesn't matter if the man cheated or
beat his wife. He's off the hook. Meanwhile, women are
left to live in shame. It's all bullshit."

Veera raises her glass. "Exactly. Which is why I
could care less about that cultural mess. I refuse to let
my parents near me on the day that is going to set the

                              The "I" in Indian

tone for the rest of my life."

She watches me carefully, waiting for my reaction. And I can't lie. She makes a damn good point. But before I can dwell on it too much, she shifts gears. "I'm actually surprised you don't already think like this. I mean— given your past."

The mere thought of not inviting my parents to my wedding makes me cringe. So, I quickly change the subject.

"Speaking of divorce... Do you think I should tell Leo about mine?"

Veera considers this, her gaze thoughtful. "Yes. Absolutely. You never know where people are going to fall on the spectrum of acceptance, and it's better to find out now rather than wait."

I nod slowly, letting her words settle. She's right. I know she's right. But that doesn't make it any less terrifying.

Later that night, back in our hotel room, I slip into the cool, expensive sheets, feeling the fabric glide against my freshly shaved legs. The city hums outside our window, the neon glow of the strip casting patterns on the walls. Veera is already asleep beside me, her breathing steady, peaceful. I should be exhausted, but my mind is restless.

Our conversation lingers, igniting an unsettling

realization. I don't really have much of a relationship with my father, either. He provided for me, and I knew I could call him in an emergency, but does he really know me? Do I really know him? And my mother: Has she ever truly seen me as a person or just as a role to be fulfilled? If I ever have kids, I won't want that kind of relationship. I will want more.

Just as I start to drift, my phone buzzes. Leo. Texting. Always so consistent.

Leo

Did you hit the jackpot yet?

A small smile tugs at my lips.

Aria

We are in bed already. Getting too old for Vegas.

A few moments pass.

Aria

Can I ask you something?

                              The "I" in Indian

Leo

Of course, princess.

I hesitate before typing.

Aria

Are you close to your father?

His response comes quickly.

Leo

**Of course. He's one of my best friends.
In fact, he'd like to meet you when you
get back.**

A mix of excitement and nerves coils in my stomach.
I reread his message, feeling something shift inside me.
This was new. Different. Maybe even something real.

I set my phone down, exhaling softly. For the first
time in a long time, I let myself believe that something
good could be waiting for me on the other side of this.

And with that thought, I finally let sleep take me.

CHAPTER 8

AN UNWELCOME TRUTH

The heat of the Las Vegas sun radiates against my skin as I lean back into the plush lounge chair at Mandalay Bay's pool, the scent of sunscreen and chlorine thick in the air. The lazy hum of conversations around us blends with the distant splash of people cooling off in the water. Veera, sprawled out next to me in her oversized sunglasses and floppy sun hat, takes a slow sip from her frozen margarita.

"You're grinning," she notes, side-eyeing me. "That's suspicious."

I smirk, setting my drink down. "Leo wants me to meet his father when I get back."

Veera lifts her sunglasses slightly, peering at me

over the rim. "Oh?"

"Yeah. And I don't know.... It just feels significant. Like, maybe this is actually something real."

Veera doesn't say anything at first. She just watches me carefully, the way only best friends do when they're trying to decide whether to let you have your moment or drag you back to reality. Finally, she exhales and shakes her head. "Look, I don't want to rain on your parade, but you need to keep your feet on the ground."

I frown. "What do you mean?"

"I mean, American guys introduce women to their parents all the time. It's not like in our culture where that's a huge deal. In our world, meeting the parents is basically a pre-engagement ceremony." She leans forward, adjusting her hat. "But Americans? Their moms are just happy their sons are dating someone who isn't a stalker or a gold digger. It's a different world, Aria. Don't get ahead of yourself is all I'm sayin'!"

I shift uncomfortably. Her words settle into my brain like an unwelcome truth. I hadn't thought of it that way. The idea of meeting someone's parents had always been ingrained in me as a monumental step—one that carries weight and expectation. But maybe, to Leo, it was just... normal? casual? The doubt creeps in, tainting the excitement I had been feeling just moments ago.

"Okay, so what are you saying?" I ask, forcing a

The "I" in Indian

laugh. "That I should go in expecting to be one of ten women they've met?"

Veera snorts. "I mean, probably not ten. But yeah... Wait," Veera peers at me. "You, like, actually like this guy, huh?"

I don't say anything, but my coyness gives away my true feelings.

"Oh, Ari, I am so happy for you," she beams. "You deserve the world."

That evening, we dress up for a dinner at the Bellagio, slipping into our best dresses—the kind that make us feel like we own the world—even if just for one night.

The restaurant is dimly lit, the kind of place where the pasta portions are tiny, but the ambiance makes up for it. As we twirl bites of linguine onto our forks, Veera leans back, tilting her glass of wine toward me. "Remember our first Vegas trip?"

I chuckle, shaking my head. "How could I forget?"

It had been Veera's birthday, a trip born from necessity rather than celebration. Veera, drowning in resentment over her father, and me, fresh out of my marriage, still reeling from the shame, the loss, the emptiness. We hadn't come to Vegas for the parties or the gambling. We had come to forget.

We never talked about that trip in detail—it was too

raw, too heavy—but we both knew what it had meant. It had saved us. It had cemented a tradition that, 10 years on, was still ours.

Veera lifts her glass higher. "To good traditions, even better friends, and overpriced cocktails."

I laugh and clink my glass against hers. "And to making it through."

The rest of the trip is a blur of poolside lounging, late-night conversations, and wedding planning. We discuss every detail of Veera's big day—from the gold embroidery on her lehenga to the garlands made of red and white carnations to the specific peacock designs in her henna.

Finally, it's time to head home. As we wait at the airport, Veera nudges me. "Next time I see you, you'll be at my wedding."

I nod, suddenly feeling the weight of how fast time is moving. "Three months."

"Three months." She squeezes my hand. "And maybe by then, you'll have figured out what's actually going on with Leo."

I smirk. "Maybe."

We hug one last time before boarding our flights. As I settle into my seat, I glance down at my phone.

I smile, typing back.

As the plane takes off, I close my eyes, exhaling slowly. Whatever happens next, this trip solidified one thing. I do like Leo—for real, for real.

CHAPTER 9

FIRST IMPRESSIONS

I've met parents before—smiled politely, complimented the food, laughed at dad jokes I didn't understand. But tonight feels...different.

This time, I realize...I care.

I grip the bottle of wine in my lap, tapping my fingers against the glass, trying to steady my thoughts. We're 10 minutes out from Leo's parents' house, and my mind is already racing through a dozen potential landmines. What if they think I'm too different? Too guarded? Too... not who they pictured?

"You okay?" Leo's hand squeezes my knee gently.

I exhale, trying to release the weight pressing on my chest. "Yeah. Just... first impressions matter, you know?"

"They do," he says, voice calm, steady. "And you're going to make a great one."

I turn to him, eyes narrowed playfully. "Okay. Rapid-fire round. Three things I should know before we get there."

He chuckles. "What is this? Our first date again?"

"Humor me."

"Alright. One: They just hit their 40th wedding anniversary. Two: Extremely progressive. Three: They love wine."

I nod, absorbing each point. "Good. Those are things I can work with." Then I pause, a new worry rising. "Wait. Should I drink in front of them?"

Leo blinks at me like I've asked whether breathing is allowed. "Well... did you bring your ID?"

I roll my eyes and smack his arm lightly. "You're not helping."

We pull into the driveway, and I take in the home. It's charming—white siding, black shutters, a modest front porch with tidy bushes. It looks exactly like the kind of place where stories begin and never quite end— the kind of place where people grow roots.

The door swings open before we can even knock.

"Welcome, Aria!" Leo's mom pulls me into a hug before I can fully register what's happening. She smells like lavender and butter.

"Oh! Hi!" I laugh, caught off-guard. But it's genuine. Warm.

She steps back, giving me a once-over like she's memorizing me. "You're even more beautiful than Leo described."

Well, so was she. Blondish, brownish hair perfectly shapes her face. Big, hazel eyes. Extremely clear skin. This woman doesn't look a day over 25. I glance at Leo, whose face is already turning red. "Mom..."

"Oh hush, Leo." She waves him off like he's an afterthought. "Come in! Dinner's almost ready."

The house smells incredible. Like roasted garlic, tomatoes, and... home.

Leo's dad appears from the kitchen, a glass of wine in hand, and a presence that fills the room without effort. He's stocky and broad, with deep green eyes that mirror Leo's. I don't need a paternity test.

"You must be Aria." He shakes my hand, then surprises me with a half-hug. "Hope you like red. Maria tells me it's the only thing civilized people drink."

I laugh, the tension in my shoulders loosening a little. "Red's my favorite."

We move into the dining room, and the table is already set—stuffed shells bubbling in a casserole dish, a salad with fresh herbs, bread still steaming. It's the kind of table that's seen laughter and arguments and late-night conversations over too many glasses of wine.

We're barely past the salad course when Leo's dad dives in.

"You won't believe the bullshit I read today," he says, shaking his head. "Maria's been working her ass off for months, going above and beyond, and guess who got the promotion?"

"Anthony..." Leo's mom sighs, clearly used to this.

"No, no. I need to say this." He turns to me. "Her boss—classic old boys' club—gave it to another white guy, same mold, same story. Maria's been running circles around them."

My eyebrows rise slightly. I glance at Maria—Leo's mom—who shrugs it off with a polite smile. "It's fine. I'm used to it."

"Used to it?" Tony scoffs. "That's exactly the problem."

It's jarring. Not because I disagree, but because this would never happen at my parents' table. We don't talk about things like this. Not with this kind of raw honesty. We just... eat. Smile. Nod. Pretend.

Maria steps in, steering the conversation like someone who's been in these waters before. "But enough about work!" She turns to me, eyes bright. "I have to admit we don't meet a lot of people from different backgrounds around here. I'd love to hear

                    The "I" in Indian

more about your family and your culture."

I hesitate. Just for a beat. It's not that I don't want to share. It's just that I never know how much people really want to hear—or if they'll only listen for the exotic bits.

"Well," I begin slowly, "my parents immigrated from India in their 20s. My mom was raised in a military family—super-structured, very formal. My dad's family was the same. They built everything from scratch here. Businesses. A home. A life."

Maria's eyes widen. "That's incredible. I can only imagine how much strength that took."

I nod. "They're traditional, though. Very focused on doing things the 'right' way, which mostly means 'their' way."

Her face softens. "We're Italian, and family is everything to us, too. It's why we watch sports together, why we celebrate even the smallest things. That's my excuse anyway. These boys are just here for the food."

She gestures to the plate in front of me. "These shells? Made from scratch. The sauce? Tomatoes from my garden."

My eyes light up. "That sounds amazing."

And just like that, she beams. Like something clicked.

That night, Leo and I curl up in bed in the kind of quiet that only comes when your nerves have finally settled.

Leo's fingers trace gentle shapes on my arm. "You okay? You got quiet when my dad talked about work."

I pause, debating how much to say. "I wasn't uncomfortable. Just... surprised. I'm not used to families talking like that. Openly. About anything."

"You mean politics?" he asks.

I laugh softly. "No. Anything. My family doesn't do heavy topics. We don't get uncomfortable. We just... exist. Float on the surface."

He tightens his hold around me. "That sounds tough."

"It's just... normal to me." I rest my head against his chest, listening to the steady thump of his heart. "But you know, as much as your dad's bluntness caught me off-guard, I kind of admire it. He says what he believes, and no one freaked out. You all just... talked."

"That's how it should be," Leo murmurs.

I close my eyes and let that settle inside me. The openness. The warmth. The possibility of something different.

Maybe this is what real belonging feels like.

Maybe this is the start of home.

CHAPTER 10
FACING FACTS

The afternoon sun streams through the window of my living room, casting golden patterns on the hardwood floor. I sit cross-legged on my desk chair, which I had repositioned near the largest window so I can stare into the one tiny courtyard in this crowded neighborhood. My thoughts are a storm, swirling faster than I can keep up with.

I have spent years believing things I hadn't chosen to believe—ideas passed down to me like family heirlooms I never wanted but couldn't discard. Notions like "Indian people marry other Indian people."

Most cultures did, to be fair. And I had tried that. I had done what was expected of me, what was ingrained in me as the "right" thing to do. When I married Arun, I thought I was following the formula for a successful life: same background, same values. A match made in cultural alignment. It was supposed to guarantee happiness, wasn't it?

But it didn't work. What use were shared traditions when we couldn't even share mutual respect?

For as long as I can remember, I'd heard the warnings, the whispers, the outright disdain: Americans have no values. Their country has a high divorce rate. Their children don't respect their elders. Those words had been drilled into me, molded into the very core of how I view the world.

Leo's family is shattering all of these ideas for me. His parents have been married for 40 freaking years—40 years of partnership, laughter, and love. I saw it in the way they speak to each other, the way they lean into each other even during quiet moments.

And Leo himself... He has values. He is deeply respectful, not just to me, but to everyone around him. He shows me love in ways that make sense to me. No grand gestures or empty words—just genuine care, attention, action. He listens, really listens, and makes me feel seen.

This isn't supposed to happen.

I am not supposed to look at his family and feel like we are alike. I am not supposed to wonder why my own upbringing had been so fixated on judging families like

                          The "I" in Indian

his. I am not supposed to question my mother's voice in my head, the voice that insists that marrying someone outside our culture is a setup for failure.

But here I am. Trying to concentrate on the redesign for a very important campaign that is set to launch in a few days. During the past few years, my magazine had to navigate a new era when most people don't read physical copies of anything anymore. Of course, we had embraced the new world of digital channels and now appear in millions of inboxes with the latest on sustainable materials and the ever-changing consumer appetite for multifunctional, stylish spaces that blend comfort with innovation. This really gave us an edge; we are now both print and digital, making our brand the best in the nation. For weeks, I have worked carefully on creating hard-hitting marketing messaging that would remind readers exactly how we dominate the furniture market. It's brilliant, if I say so myself. I wish I could carry this confidence into the decision-making in my romantic life. Isn't it funny that a woman can be so confident when it comes to her career, but that same woman can be so lost when it comes to love?

It isn't about culture, is it? Culture is just a shared set of norms, which can exist among so many different groups. It is not about race. Good people and bad people exist everywhere. Values aren't exclusive to one race.

They aren't stamped onto a passport or encoded into DNA.

So why can't my parents see that? Why couldn't I see it until now?

No matter how many logical arguments I make to myself, the doubt remains. That ever-present, gnawing doubt that my mother's voice had planted in me long ago. Her words live rent-free in my mind, echoing with a cruel certainty:

What if you're wrong? What if you're being naïve again? What if you get hurt again?

I had been duped before. By Arun, by the life I thought we'd build together. It had left me raw and wary, convinced I need to protect myself at all costs.

And now here I am—caught between the safety of my mother's ingrained fears and the dangerous allure of Leo's family life—something new, something different, something that might actually be right.

My phone buzzes, pulling me from my thoughts. Saira.

I pick up, barely getting a hello in before she launches into a frustrated rant.

"They're driving me crazy, Ari. I swear to God, if I don't get some space from them, I might scream."

I sigh, rubbing my forehead. "Mom and Dad?"

"No, the Queen of England," she shoots back,

                                    The "I" in Indian

exasperated. "Yes, Mom and Dad. You'd think they are the ones in residency, the way they are hovering over me lately. Mom keeps bringing up marriage proposals from 'such nice boys from such good families,' and Dad keeps dropping hints about his friend who has a son that is also a doctor in Colorado."

"Yikes," I mutter.

"Exactly." Saira sighs. "So, tell me something that doesn't involve our parents before I lose my mind."

I hesitate for a moment, then decide—why not? "I met Leo's parents."

Silence.

Then, "You what?"

"I met his parents."

"Like... met met? Like, sat down and had a meal with them?"

"Yes, Saira."

She let out a sharp breath. "Ari... what are you doing?"

"What do you mean?"

"You know what I mean. This relationship. What's your plan here?"

I felt my body tense. "What kind of question is that?"

"I mean, what's the end game? It's not like our family is ever going to agree to you marrying a white boy."

I swallow hard.

"Aria," she says, voice softer now, "I love seeing you happy. I do. But meeting his parents? Don't you think you might be wasting your time?"

I feel something hot rise in my chest—defensiveness, maybe anger. "Why? We're American, too. If they didn't want us to meet American men, then why raise us here?"

Saira is quiet for a long moment. When she finally speaks, her voice is resigned. "I don't have an answer for you. I just know how it is."

"And aren't you tired of it? Of pretending? Don't you ever want to challenge what we were taught?" I pushed. "Aren't you tired of living someone else's idea of what your life should be?"

"Oh, Ari..." she sighs. "Not everyone has the energy to swim against the tide. I barely have enough energy to get through my residency. I don't have any extra to fight Mom and Dad on top of it."

I clench my jaw, my frustration brewing.

Saira continues, her voice gentle now. "I just think... before you get too deep, think about the big picture. And while you're at it, you need to tell Leo about your divorce."

I exhale, the reminder pressing down on me.

Saira adds, "For all we know, telling him might solve the situation for you. Who knows if he'll even want to keep dating after that?"

A hollow feeling settles in my chest. "So, you think this is a moot point?"

"I think it's something you need to find out."

The days blur together as I fall deeper into this spiral, this...funk. My carefully constructed beliefs are being deconstructed before my eyes, and I don't know how to stop it.

I stare at my now-cold tea, my grip tightening around the mug.

There is no escaping it now. I have to tell him.

CHAPTER 11
TITLE

Aria

Can you meet this evening?

Leo

Miss me huh?

Aria

I was hoping we could talk.

Leo

Perfect, because there's something I want to discuss with you too. See you tonight.

I'm nursing an IPA at the sleek, oval bar, waiting for our bay at Top Golf. It's buzzing tonight—Friday crowds, retro lights, and Ariana Grande blaring over the speakers. This isn't the typical driving range I grew up with, but I like it. Modern, fun, and a little over the top—just like dating in 2025.

Aria's late, and it's making me nervous. Normally, I'd brush it off. But tonight feels different. She's been a little distant this week, and I can't help but worry. My leg bounces restlessly on the barstool as I scroll through ESPN, though I'm not really paying attention. I know she has that big campaign at work that's been taking up her time, so I'm trying not to overthink it.

Shooting golf balls is exactly what I need right now after a long week of school. School kids have a way of monopolizing your brain cells, leaving little room for much else. They cry over everything: if they accidentally trip and fall, if they can't do something they want to do, if they miss a goal, or even if they see other kids crying. Sometimes, I think they cry just because they can. And, as much as I love my job, I need to blow off some steam.

Aria has to know how much I'm into her. I mean, I daydream about her constantly—our next date, the way she laughs, the way her lips taste like strawberries. If she doesn't feel that by now, I'm obviously screwing this up.

The hostess interrupts my spiral to let me know our bay

                                    The "I" in Indian

is ready. I grab my beer and head over, trying to shake the nerves. I look around and notice the setup is ridiculously fancy—black marble floors, sectional sofas, electronic ball machines, even a space heater for cold nights. A full bar. When did driving ranges become so fancy? But I'm here for it, and the fact that Aria chose this place proves how well she gets me.

I grab a pitching wedge, fall into my stance, and swing, sending the ball sailing. There's something meditative about the rhythm of golf. It's one of the few things that quiets my mind—until I hear her voice.

"125 yards. Not bad, champ!"

I turn to see Aria strolling toward me, her eyes sparkling with amusement. She's radiant tonight, her athletic tights hugging her curves and her hair spilling over her shoulders like silk. Her teasing immediately puts me at ease.

"How'd you know how far it went?" I ask, still caught off-guard by her beauty.

She points to the giant screen above the bay. "They put chips in the balls to track them. Pretty cool, huh?"

Of course they do. Fancy shit.

I meet her halfway, pulling her close for a quick kiss on the cheek. It's been a week since I last saw her, but it feels like forever. "Hi," I say softly, inhaling the faint scent of her vanilla perfume.

"Hi," she replies, her lips curling into a smile that's this shy of mischievous. "Are you ready to get your ass kicked at some golf?"

I smirk, handing her the club. "Do you even know what to do with this?"

She doesn't dignify me with a response, just waves me off as she takes her place at the mat. I sink into the plush sofa, watching her every move. She grips the club confidently, her stance impeccable.

When she swings, the ball soars, and we both look at the screen—116 yards. Damn.

"Okay, so you can play golf. What else are you hiding from me?" I tease, but the light in her eyes dims slightly. She walks over, setting the club aside, and takes a seat on the sofa—too far from me for my liking.

"Maybe this is a good time for us to talk," she says, her voice quieter now.

My chest tightens. This is it. She's about to tell me she's done with me.

"So, there's something I've been meaning to talk to you about," she starts, but I cut her off.

"Wait," I say, leaning forward. "Before you say anything, I have something I need to ask you."

Her brow furrows in confusion, but she nods. "Okay. What is it?"

I take a deep breath, my pulse racing. "I care about you so much that I haven't been able to stop thinking about you.

   The "I" in Indian

That's why… I booked us a trip. A week at the beach as soon as school lets out. The hotel's paid for, and I planned a bunch of stuff—massages, water excursions, the works. Will you come with me?"

Her eyes widen, and, for a moment, she just stares at me. I can't tell if she's about to smile or tell me I'm insane.

Finally, she nods, a slow smile spreading across her face. "Okay," she says softly.

Relief washes over me, and I realize that I've been holding my breath. "Okay?" I repeat, grinning like an idiot.

"Okay," she says again, leaning in closer. "But I still plan to kick your ass at golf."

CHAPTER 12

THE PERFECT DAY

The drive into the city is starting to feel like second nature. Route 50—winding past sprawling horse farms and picture-perfect landscapes—has become my favorite stretch of road. Funny, I've driven this route a hundred times before, but it never felt this beautiful. Maybe it's not the drive; it's where I'm going—or who I'm going to.

My family jokes that I'm terrible at answering my phone, but, these days, I wake up waiting for it to ring. Aria calls every morning without fail, walking me through her day: big design meetings, editorial reviews, press releases that have to get out by the deadline. She's wicked smart and always juggling a million things. All I want to do is take some of it off her plate. Let her breathe. Let her know she's not alone.

That's why this weekend getaway matters so much to me. The beach, just an hour away, feels like the perfect escape. She called earlier in a flurry, panicking over not having an umbrella or sunscreen. I couldn't help but laugh. "I've got you," I told her. And I meant it. Two chairs, an umbrella, sunscreen, towels, snacks, drinks—I packed everything. Hell, I even brought boogie boards. If nothing else, I'm going to prove that she can count on me.

The truth is, I've never felt this way about anyone before. I've dated, sure, but it always felt like I was going through the motions. With Aria, it's different. She makes me want to show up, to be better. Maybe I should tell her that.

I picked her up, and we have been on the road for about 20 minutes when I reach for my phone to cue up some music. "Any requests?" I ask.

"Nothing too intense," she says, leaning back in her seat. "It's a beach day, after all."

I grin, scrolling through my playlists. I land on one labeled Road Trip Classics and hit play. The first song is Springsteen's *Born to Run*. I crank it up and start drumming on the steering wheel.

Aria listens for a moment, her expression thoughtful. "I don't think I've ever heard this one before," she says.

I glance at her, startled. "What? This is Springsteen. The Boss! How have you never heard this?"

She shrugs, her face half-apologetic, half-amused. "I don't know. I guess I just missed it."

"You were born here, right?" I ask, chuckling.

"Yes," she says, laughing now. "But, you have to understand; my parents are Indian immigrants. I grew up with Bollywood soundtracks and old Hindi classics playing in the car. My grandparents only spoke Hindi, and the TV was always tuned to Indian channels. I didn't really get exposed to American music until high school."

"High school?!" I exclaim. "So, what? You just skipped the '70s, '80s, and '90s music canon entirely?"

"Pretty much," she admits, smiling. "Until I discovered my own taste, I just listened to whatever my parents liked. And trust me, it wasn't Springsteen."

I shake my head in mock disbelief. "I feel like I don't even know you."

She laughs, swatting my arm. "Oh, come on. It's not that bad."

"It's worse than bad. It's tragic." I scroll through the playlist, trying to find a song she might recognize. "Okay, what about Fleetwood Mac? Tom Petty? Billy Joel?"

She shakes her head at each name, and I groan dramatically. "Aria, this is... this is cultural malpractice. I can't let this stand."

"Well, educate me, Mr. Roselli," she says, crossing her arms with a smirk.

Challenge accepted. I keep scrolling, determined to find common ground. Finally, I land on something that feels universal. "The Beatles. Please tell me you know The

Beatles."

Her face lights up. "Of course, I know The Beatles. Who doesn't?"

"Thank God," I say, pressing play. The opening chords of *Here Comes the Sun* fill the car, and she starts humming along.

By the time we get to the chorus, we're both singing at the top of our lungs, her voice blending with mine in an off-key but joyful harmony. The tension from earlier melts away, replaced by something warm and easy.

"This," she says, pointing at the stereo, "this I can get behind."

"Well, it's a start," I say, grinning.

The beach is quieter than I expected—the ocean stretching out endlessly under a cloudless sky. We set up close to the water, just far enough from the teenagers playing volleyball to avoid their stray balls and noise. Aria sinks into her chair, burying her feet in the sand, her face softening as she stares out at the waves.

Then, the wind shifts.

At first, it's subtle, a slight coolness against my skin. But then the sand starts whipping, and Aria shields her face, squinting against the sudden gust. I look up and see the clouds rolling in fast, darkening the sky.

"Uh... was this in the forecast?" she asks, her voice raised over the wind.

"Nope."

The first fat raindrop splatters onto my arm. Then another. The storm crashes over us in seconds. The wind rips the umbrella straight from the sand, sending it tumbling toward the waves.

"Leo!" Aria yelps, scrambling up.

I dart after it, but the wind is stronger. Within moments, it's gone.

I grab our bags, my jaw tight as we sprint back to the hotel, soaked and breathless. This was supposed to be perfect. I wanted her to see that I had everything under control, that she could count on me. And now? I lost the umbrella. Idiot.

We step into the hotel room, dripping onto the tile. I drag a hand through my wet hair, frustrated. "I should have checked the forecast. I should've anchored the umbrella better. This whole weekend was supposed to be..."

A sound stops me. Laughter. Aria is laughing, full and unrestrained, her whole body shaking. She leans against the door, gasping between fits of giggles.

I blink at her. "You're laughing?"

She nods, trying to catch her breath. "Leo, you..." she wheezes, pointing at me. "You look so serious, like you are trying to single-handedly battle nature itself." She clutches her stomach. "It was just an umbrella!"

I exhale, the tension dissolving. And then, just like that, I see her. Not just her smile or the way she looks at me, but what she does to me. How she softens every sharp edge. How she makes everything feel lighter, easier.

I love her.

The realization hits me like the storm outside. And for once, I don't try to fight it.

CHAPTER 13

GATHERING CLOUDS

Saira

Have you told him yet?

Aria

No.

Saira

What are you waiting for?

Aria

I really like him. I don't want this to end.

Saira

It might not.

The following evening, the storm was a memory, leaving behind a beach breeze, perfect for a nice boardwalk stroll. Leo gives me dibs on the bathroom to get ready, and I can hear him flipping through TV channels outside. I braid one side of my hair and curl the other side, looking beachy. I just need to get dressed now. I've packed way more than necessary—a daily outfit for my inner stripper and another for my inner saint. I pull out a skin-tight jean skirt and a crop top, throwing them on and eyeing myself in the mirror. I can totally wear this. My boobs look perky, my stomach flat. But as I admire myself, a flashback creeps in—one I'd rather forget.

It was many summers ago. I was lounging poolside at a private neighborhood pool. It was a small pool, meant only for the people in our small condo

The "I" in Indian

community. It was the middle of the day, so the pool was completely empty. Desperately needing a break from my laptop, I ventured out there with a Nora Roberts book, wearing a peach-and-black-striped bikini that I'd bought at Victoria's Secret. As I was slipping into the peace of sun and solitude, Arun, my then-husband, called to ask where I was. He sometimes came home for a quick lunch. I casually told him. A mistake.

I remember him stomping toward me, the booming voice, the cutting put-downs, the berating of my swimwear all the way home. I clutched a towel around myself, begging him to lower his voice so the neighbors wouldn't hear. The humiliation of being scolded, of feeling exposed, of being made to believe I'd done something wrong — just because I wore a bikini in public. I recall the bargaining, trying to make him understand that bikinis were common at the pool. Everyone wears them. No, one was even there. I remember the sinking feeling when he told me that I was not living up to his expectations for a wife.

I shake the memory off, but it makes me reconsider today's outfit choice. This is our first trip together. The last thing I want is for Leo to think I'm inappropriate or unpresentable. I change into a long white maxi dress, cute but conservative. I can save the sexy stuff for later. We head to the lobby. Leo reaches for my hand as we pass by the check-in counter. The automatic doors slide open right onto the boardwalk, and we head toward the carnival a few blocks down. We pass by surf shops, tiki bars, and an occasional busker. The distant sound of the waves is peaceful, but my mind is anything but peaceful.

I know I should tell Leo about my divorce. The weekend has been nearly perfect, and I selfishly don't want to ruin it. It's not like I'm lying to him; I just haven't shared one of the most defining parts of my life. Isn't that normal?

Honestly, I've never understood the fuss about being divorced. Sure, people vow to stay together forever, but things change. If circumstances brought two people together and they were happy for a while, does that mean they should stay miserable later? What if someone becomes abusive or neglectful? My mom would say they should stay together—always, no matter what. She's a better woman than me, I guess.

But it makes me wonder: How many women stay in unhappy marriages because they're taught love is unconditional? Are they truly happy, or have they surrendered to their circumstances? To me, love should have conditions—mutual respect, care, and honoring each other. If those are gone, why should divorce be off the table?

Breaking the silence, I ask, "Do you believe in

                                        The "I" in Indian

divorce?"

Leo looks surprised. "No. I don't."

His confident tone makes my stomach drop. "Like...
under any circumstances?"

"Nope. I think, once you're married, you work
through your issues. Otherwise, you're a quitter."

I freeze. My hand stays in his, but I feel paralyzed.

"What's up?" he asks, turning toward me.

If he doesn't believe in divorce, will he ever
understand my past? Will he judge me or walk away? I
almost tell him, but the words catch in my throat. He's
looking for someone who doesn't believe in divorce,
who sees love as unconditional. And here I am, divorced,
"damaged goods," a firm believer that love should have
conditions.

"I think my legs are tired from walking. Can we
head back to the hotel?" I say.

Leo nods, pulling my hand closer to his arm,
wrapping it around his bicep. He keeps his hand on
mine for the entire walk. He doesn't ask me why I
brought up divorce. Isn't he curious? Or maybe I'm just
insecure.

As we get back to the hotel room, I jet into the
bathroom, needing a moment to gather myself. I glance
over at the sexy outfit I was hoping to put on for Leo
tonight, but I don't think I can. I feel sick and panicked.

If I get too intimate with him, I think I might start crying. So, I come out in the least sexy outfit I packed—a pair of oversized sweatpants and a baggy shirt.

Leo is sitting on the edge of the bed, the dim hotel light casting a beautiful glow on his dimple. His face lights up when he looks at me, "You somehow manage to look beautiful even in sweatpants," he says with an adorable smile that weakens my knees.

I smile back but keep my distance. He suddenly gets up, putting on his shoes. "I need to grab something really quick. Hold on to this," he says, handing me my phone.

I glance at the clock. It's 10:30 pm. Where could he possibly be going at this hour? Before I can ask, he's out the door.

I slump into bed, pulling the covers over my head. My mother's words echo in my mind: "Divorce matters to people." She might be right.

The phone rings. It's Leo. "Come out to the balcony," he says and hangs up.

I drag myself out, unsure of how long he's been gone. The night is so clear I can see the stars. The moon lights up the sand below. I squint at the beach, unsure of what I'm looking for. And then I see it: I LOVE YOU ARIA written in the sand in massive letters. Leo stands in front of it, hands in his pockets like a shy schoolboy,

                    The "I" in Indian

grinning ear to ear.

I stare, stuck. How did he do this? We're on the 7th
floor. Those letters must be massive for me to be able
to see them from up here. This might be the sweetest,
most romantic thing anyone has ever done for me. But,
instead of feeling joy, my gut twists. Leo doesn't deserve
this. How did I let it get to this point without telling
him the truth? I hadn't even considered that my silence
could break his heart, too.

Tears spill down my cheeks as I turn and retreat
inside, leaving him out there alone in the sand.

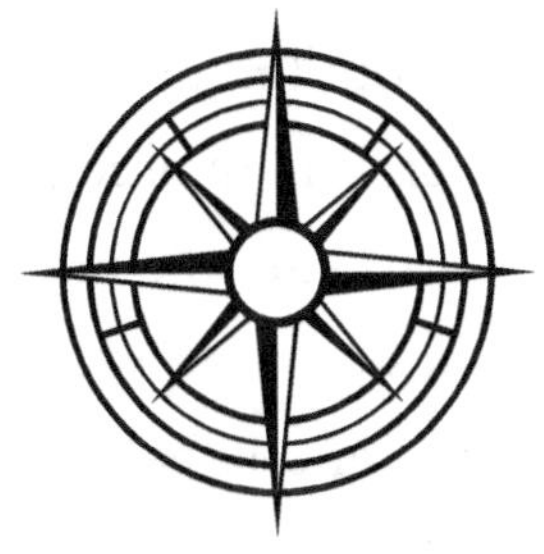

CHAPTER 14
STORM BREAK

I'm waiting for the elevator to reach the 7th floor. OMG. It's taking forever. My patience is wearing thin. Damn. I need to get upstairs. The last thing I wanted was to make Aria cry. I abandon the elevator and take the stairs, skipping steps two at a time. By the time I reach the 7th floor, I'm out of breath but fueled by adrenaline. I swing the room door open to find Aria packing her things.

"Are you leaving?" I ask, confused and panicked.

She doesn't answer.

"Listen, if I freaked you out by saying I love you too soon, I'm sorry. We can slow things down. That wasn't my intention..."

She cuts me off, raising her hand. Her face is streaked with tears, her shoulders trembling. "Just stop, Leo."

"Aria, why are you crying? Will you tell me what's going

on?" My voice is too loud, but I'm desperate to understand.

Finally, she explodes. "I'm divorced, OK?!" Her hands fly up in frustration. Her words stun me into silence. "Damaged goods. One of the bad ones. Couldn't work things out. A big 'quitter'." Her voice cracks, and it feels like she's spitting out the words she's been choking on. "So, just move out of the way, and let me go."

She keeps moving—folding clothes, shoving them into her suitcase, avoiding my eyes.

I try to process what she said. Divorced? Damaged goods? A quitter? None of it makes sense to me. I've never seen her like this—so frantic, so raw. I want to reach out, to pull her into a hug, but I'm frozen.

"Aria..." I finally manage. "Wait. Can we talk about this? You don't have to..."

But before I can finish, she brushes past me, suitcase in hand, and walks out of the room.

I'm left standing there, staring at the door. What the fuck just happened?

CHAPTER 15
RIDE OF SHAME

I lug my suitcase down the gravelly sidewalk, the wheels catching on rocks as I struggle to keep my balance in my sandals, my cardigan halfway hanging off my shoulder. The evening sky has faded into complete darkness, a sharp contrast to the whirlwind of emotions swirling inside me. My chest is tight, my heart pounding.

The Uber pulls up, a sleek, black sedan that seems far too calm and composed for the chaotic mess I feel inside. I open the trunk and heave my suitcase into it with more force than necessary, before sliding into the backseat. The driver offers a polite nod into the rearview mirror.

"Aria?" he asks.

I nod in agreement and climb in, barely able to meet his eyes.

The app displays the estimated fare: $282. I stare at the number, as if it is mocking me. If that isn't the clearest sign that I have made an impulsive choice, I don't know what is.

The car starts moving, and I lean my head back against the seat, trying to calm the storm in my mind. My chest feels heavy, like a weight is pressing down on it. I can't slow my thoughts.

What did I just do?

Images of Leo's concerned face flash through my mind. His brow furrowed, his green eyes searching mine for answers I didn't give him. I didn't even give him a chance to respond. I just...bolted. The memory of him standing there, helpless, as I stormed out of the hotel room, make my stomach churn.

I press my forehead against the cool window, watching the lights of passing cars blur into streaks of white and red. My reflection stares back at me, pale and frazzled, the weight of my impulsive decision written all over my face.

My phone buzzes in my lap, jolting me out of my thoughts. It's Leo. Of course.

The screen lights up with his name and my favorite picture of him. My heart twists painfully. He calls. Once.

     The "I" in Indian

Twice. Three times.

Each time, I hit decline, my thumb trembling as I do.

He didn't do anything wrong. I am not even mad at him. I am embarrassed. Embarrassed by my own behavior, by how I had let my emotions take over, by how I had completely unraveled in front of him. I wasn't calm enough to face him, to explain myself, to even begin to make things right.

I let out a shaky breath, my mind racing back to the hotel room. The way I had lashed out, my words spilling out in a flurry of anger and insecurity before I grabbed my things and ran. I recognize it now for what it was—a classic fight-or-flight response. And I had chosen flight.

Self-sabotage, plain and simple.

My phone buzzes again—this time with a text. I hesitate, my chest tightening as I open it.

Leo

I know you're upset. You can be as upset as you want. But I need to know you're safe.

His words hit me like a punch to the gut. Despite my terrible behavior, despite the way I'd stormed out without giving him a chance, he is still thinking about me. He cares about my safety.

My vision blurs as tears well up. Isn't this what I'd always wanted? Someone who knew what is truly important, who could see through the chaos and still care? Someone who could accept me, even at my worst?

I type back a quick response, my hands shaking as I hit send.

I set my phone down and lean my head back against the seat, staring out the window. The tears come then, hot and heavy, spilling over my face as the weight of everything crashes down on me.

I want to call Veera. She would know exactly what to say to pull me back from the abyss. But the last thing I want to do is bother her—not when she is knee-deep in wedding plans, moving her own life forward while mine unravels.

Instead, I close my eyes and let myself remember when we celebrated her big move to California.

It was about two years ago. She had just got the call that would change the course of her career. After years of slaving in government contracting, bouncing from one consulting contractor to another, she had finally heard from Google. She had landed her dream job—managing IT projects for the world's biggest and most forward-thinking innovation company.

We decided to have our last hurrah at our college stomping grounds, The Bad Rose. We had spent countless nights there during our younger, carefree days. The place hadn't changed much—dark, sticky floors, a long bar cluttered with drunk college kids, early 2000s music blaring so loudly you could barely talk to each other.

Veera ordered her signature whiskey sour, and I stuck with my usual vodka soda. She raised her glass for a toast, her face glowing under the neon lights.

"Well," she said with a smirk, "it's been one hell of a ride, hasn't it, A? I fucking did it!"

I raised my glass, my lips twitching into a smile. "It sure has, V. So, so proud of you and excited for your next chapter!"

She grinned, clinking her glass against mine. "Here's to always remembering our worth and to only giving up our heart when we find someone who values it as much as we value each other. Cheers!"

"Cheers," I echoed, our glasses ringing with the promise of solidarity.

After that, we'd hugged—one of those rare, tight embraces when neither of us cared who was watching. It was one of those moments that had stuck with me, one I carried with me when I needed a reminder of my own strength.

My eyes stung with tears as the memory faded, giving way to the present. Veera's words echo in my mind, a bittersweet reminder of how far I have come—and how much farther I still have to go.

I thought of Leo—of his patience, his kindness, his steady presence in my life. For the first time in years, I felt like I'd found someone who truly valued me. Someone worthy of my heart.

And I'd just royally screwed it up.

CHAPTER 16

THE CLEAREST MIRROR

I hear the knock at the door and ignore it, sinking deeper into the couch. If I don't answer, maybe they will go away.

A small part of me hopes it is Leo.

But I know better.

The knock comes again, followed by the sound of a key turning in the lock. Saira.

I barely have the energy to lift my head as she steps inside, pausing in the doorway as she takes in the disaster zone I have created. Takeout containers litter the coffee table. A half-empty bottle of wine sits next to an untouched glass. My blanket is wrapped around me like a cocoon, and I haven't even bothered to turn the lights on.

She wrinkles her nose. "Um...when was the last time you showered?"

I groan, pulling the blanket over my face. "Not in the mood, Saira."

She carefully navigates the minefield of old food containers and plops down onto the edge of the couch.

"I haven't heard from you in a week." Her voice is softer now but laced with concern. "I am worried."

I don't answer.

She places a hand on my leg, waiting. She knows me well enough to know that I will talk when I am ready.

Minutes pass. Then, finally, the words spill out. "I think I screwed up."

Saira sighs, rubbing my leg briefly before shoving my feet to the ground. "That's fine, but why don't you go take a shower first? Then, we'll talk."

I groan again.

She doesn't budge.

"Come on, Aria." She stands up, hauling me up with her. "You smell."

I let the scalding water hit my skin, washing away the week of self-pity I have been wallowing in.

For days, I have been stuck in autopilot. Wake up. Check email. Pretend to be paying attention in meetings. Order takeout. Drink wine. Watch mindless

The "I" in Indian

action movies until I pass out on the couch. Repeat.

I replay the trip over and over in my mind, dissecting every moment. Not only did I unravel in front of Leo, but I abandoned him.

And the worst part? He had not even rejected me.

I stare at my reflection in the fogged-up mirror, gripping the sink. Coward.

When I step onto the balcony, Saira is comfortably lounging on the sectional sofa with a cup of tea in her hands. It could be the hottest day of the year and us Indians would still be drinking our hot tea.

I sit down across from her, cradling my own cup, craving her usual calm reassurance that I am not the absolute worst person alive.

"So," she says, taking a sip. "How was the beach?"

I sigh, staring into my tea. "The beach was great. We lounged under the sun, played mini golf along the water. Oh, and Leo told me he loves me in the most romantic way possible."

Her brows shoot up. "Wait, what? He told you he loves you? Aria, that's..."

I shift uncomfortably. "And then, I had a meltdown,

stormed out of the hotel, and took an Uber home."

Her expression immediately flattens. "Ah. There it is. Now all of this makes more sense," she says, swirling her tea.

I glare at her. "Glad you're amused."

Saira sets her tea down. "So, what exactly caused this meltdown?"

I hesitate before answering. "He told me he doesn't believe in divorce—that he thinks people who get divorced are quitters."

Her brows knit together. "That was his reaction to hearing your story?"

I shake my head. "No. That was just his general opinion on divorce."

She tilts her head. "Okay... but did you actually tell him your story?"

I swallowed hard. "No."

A slow blink. A long sip of tea.

The silence is far more clear than anything she could have said.

I shift in my seat. "Say something."

Saira sighs, setting her cup down with a soft clink. "So, let me get this straight. He didn't say he wouldn't date you because you're divorced. He told you he loves you. And you... didn't even tell him your story?"

I nod, feeling smaller by the second.

"So, what's the problem?"

"The problem is that I completely spiraled, and now it's over."

Saira gives me a look—the kind that says "I call bullshit" without her needing to say it out loud.

"Honestly, Ari. I know I have given you a hard time about Leo, but this is something else. This is about the way you see yourself. It sounds like the only person who needs to accept you... is you."

Her words hit like a freight train.

She leans forward, her voice softer now. "You carry around the fact that you're divorced like it's a scarlet letter—like you're permanently damaged because of it. But you're not."

I let out a bitter laugh. "Maybe not to you. But to our parents? To the world?"

Saira's expression doesn't waver. "Forget them for a second. What about you? You keep telling yourself that this one thing defines your entire worth. But Aria, that's not who you are."

Her words settle in my chest, heavy but true.

I look away. "I don't know how to let it go."

She exhales. "Then, maybe you need to go to the source."

I frown. "What?"

She shrugs. "If you need Mom and Dad's approval

to finally be at peace with it, then get it. Have the conversation."

I swallow hard. The thought alone makes my stomach churn.

Saira continues, "Look, I'll be honest. I don't think you have a future with Leo."

I flinch.

She lifts a hand. "I'm just saying, I don't think this is going to end the way you want it to. And I don't want you setting yourself up for heartache. But that's a separate issue."

I look at her warily. "What's the other issue?"

She leans back in her chair, crossing her arms. "You. You're still waiting for someone else to tell you that you're enough. First, it was Arun, then Mom and Dad, now Leo. When does it end?"

I sit in stunned silence.

Saira sighs, "Aria, I love you. I don't care that you're divorced. You're still my sister, and I think you're incredible. So, I'm not totally surprised that someone else could love you, too."

I stare at her, blinking back unexpected tears.

She hesitates before adding, "But I need you to love you."

And just like that, the dam inside me cracks.

Saira, who has spent her life being the perfect

　　　　　　　　The "I" in Indian

daughter, who doesn't have the strength to live her own truth—loves me anyway.

Maybe she is right. Maybe I need to love me, too.

I stare out at the horizon, the tea in my hands growing cold.

Her words linger in the air, wrapping around me like a truth I have spent too long avoiding.

I want so badly to be accepted—by my parents, by Leo, by the world.

But maybe self-acceptance has to come first.

And, for the first time in a long time, I feel ready to try.

CHAPTER 17
MEMORIES

My mother had called me, saying she had found shoeboxes full of my old college photos that I definitely wanted. I know we need to talk, so I take the opportunity to get over there. Not 100% sure of what I am going to say, but just getting there is a step in the right direction. The scent of dusty boxes wafts through the air as I sit cross-legged on her living room floor, shuffling through old memories. My mom sits next to me, carefully watching as I sort photos into piles.

"Ten years," I think, as I hold up a photo of me on Veera's shoulders, both of us in matching blue and gold Bhangra costumes. I can't believe it has been a decade since those nights spent practicing choreography—spins, jumps, and squats—the school auditorium alive with the banging of the dhol and laughter as our

Bhangra team prepared for competitions. Back then, life felt vibrant and full of possibility.

I was about 22 in this photo, on the cusp of graduation and having secured a job in public relations at a nonprofit I'd interned with for three years. Everything seemed perfect back then. Sometimes, I wished I had never joined the dance team. But, now, looking at the bright smiles in these photos, I see that it did make me happy—at one time.

As a freshman in a new college, my parents urged me to quickly find other Indian people, saying that I'd feel more at home once I found my "people." I had always been a good dancer, having spent many a night copying popular Bollywood dance routines and performing at family parties. I was excited to connect with my roots and do something I was good at. Bhangra was a traditional village dance that had gained popularity in the 2000s and was now a competitive sport. Most universities had Bhangra teams, each comprised of 8 girls and 8 boys, that competed against each other. It was a fun way to keep traditions alive.

And that's where I met Veera Singh.

     The "I" in Indian

Veera was unlike anyone I had ever met. Short, wavy black hair, a striking smile, and with glasses that made her look bright and bubbly, Veera radiated confidence that drew people to her like moths to a flame.

As I walked onto the stage to audition, I heard someone from the peanut gallery crack a joke that I was an ABCD (an American-Born Confused Desi). Veera shot a dangerous look toward the heckler and yelled, "Be respectful to the people auditioning here, or get the fuck out!" She had been born in India but carried none of the judgment that others on the team did. She was bold and unapologetic in ways that shocked and inspired me.

After my audition, Veera approached me as I walked off the stage. "Your form is really good," she said, her voice brimming with energy. "Where's your family from?"

"Delhi," I replied hesitantly.

Her eyes lit up. "Hindi aati hai?" she asked, wondering if I could speak the mother tongue. I could and said, "Haan, bohot aache se" ("Yes, he is very good.")

"So much for being an ABCD. Welcome to the team, Aria." Veera gave me a wide grin before skipping off to join the others.

From that moment on, Veera became my anchor on

the team. She didn't just accept me; she made me feel like I belonged. She introduced me to the dance style, the traditions, and the intricate steps of folk dances I'd only seen on TV.

Being on a dance team was no small commitment. We practiced every night after class, creating audition videos to submit to competitions. One night after a late practice, Veera and I sat on the steps outside the auditorium, talking about everything from choreography to class to life. That was when she rolled up her sleeves and showed me her latest tattoo—an intricate design that illustrated her dual identity of being Indian and American.

"You have tattoos?" I asked, my jaw nearly dropping. Tattoos weren't exactly acceptable in our culture.

"Yup," she said, laughing at my reaction. "And I love every single one of them."

"But how do you hide them from your parents?" I asked, genuinely baffled.

"Why would I?" she shot back. "They know. They hate it, but I don't care. It's my body." She leaned back, exhaling as if to punctuate her statement. "Life's too short to live by my parent's rules, Aria."

Veera didn't care what anyone thought—about anything and, most especially, about her. It was clear

                              The "I" in Indian

she had gone through something that had made her this way, but I never pried. I admired her courage to live authentically, even if I wasn't ready to follow in her footsteps.

For the next few years, we won titles all around the country—and bonded quite a bit in the process. Everyone on the team knew Veera and I would be rooming together whenever we traveled for a competition.

Being on the stage was such a rush. Every time we won, we celebrated—hard. It was our senior year now, and we needed to make it count.

A few weeks into being on the team, a stranger had requested an audition. His name was Arun.

Arun was tall, dark, handsome, and fit. How had I never seen this guy at school before? We were weeks into the semester, and he had missed the year's official auditions by a lot. We already had enough people on the team, so there was some hesitation about allowing someone new to join the team this late. Remembering how hard it was for me to find belonging and break into a new group, I urged our team captains to let him at least audition, secretly hoping to spend more time with him. Idiot.

Arun was confident, charming, and a natural leader. He was the kind of guy you couldn't ignore. At first,

I only saw him as a friend. We spent hours practicing routines, laughing over inside jokes, and teasing each other during water breaks. But as the school year drew to a close, something shifted. Arun began walking me home after practice, sending late-night texts, and paying attention in ways that felt... different.

Our last big competition was in Pittsburgh— "Bhangra in the Burgh." We had spent weeks perfecting our formations, making sure every hand, finger, and head nod was aligned. We dressed in our traditional Punjabi uniforms (baby blue salwar kameez with white scarves decorated in gold polka dots).

Feeling rather emotional as I got on the stage— knowing this would probably be my last time performing for many years to come—I glanced over at Veera. She mouthed, "Let's fucking go!" This was it—time to leave it all on the stage. The lights turned on, the dhol started to thump, and I kicked into a high energy that lasted all the way through. The crowd roared, jumping to their feet to give us a standing ovation. I knew, as we posed for the finale, that we were taking the trophy home.

As we headed backstage to wait for the judges' decision, Arun pulled me aside. "I like you, Aria," he said, his voice steady. "I always thought that a strong marriage is based on a solid friendship, and you've become my best friend. I want to celebrate this win by asking you an important question. Will you marry me?"

I stood there, shocked. I had not expected that at all. On the one hand, I did like Arun. He was a good friend. On paper, he was everything my parents would have wanted—cultured, Indian, decent. On the other hand, we had not even dated. But then again, that is how people did it in this culture, wasn't it? At least, he is making his intentions clear; he doesn't just want to date me for shits and giggles but instead wants to marry me. That's bold, right?

In any case, one of my favorite Bollywood stories— one of everyone's favorite Bollywood stories—was that of Rahul and Anjali, wasn't it? A "best friends as lovers" story. Yes, I would have my very own Kuch Kuch Hota Hai love story come to life. Arun was my Rahul. I nodded, "Yes," just as they announced that we had won. He grabbed my hand and pulled me out to the stage with our team. Veera found me in the crowd, hugging me as we jumped up and down, not necessarily celebrating the same thing.

My parents were absolutely thrilled about the news. Arun was perfect in their eyes—from a good family, deeply rooted in Indian culture, and ready to take me off their hands. But not everyone was happy about my engagement. Veera approached me on the day of our graduation, her usual brightness dimmed.

"Are you sure about this, Aria?" she asked, her tone
unusually serious.

"Of course," I said, surprised by her question. "Why
wouldn't I be?"

"It's just... it's so soon," she said carefully. "You
barely know him. And, in my experience, Indian men..."
She paused, choosing her words carefully. "Let's just say
they're not always what they seem."

I bristled at her words. "Arun's not like that," I
snapped. "He's kind, supportive, and...."

"Okay," she said, holding up her hands. "I'm just
saying, 'Be careful'."

Her words stayed with me, but I didn't want to hear
them. How could Veera, my best friend, doubt Arun?
It felt like a betrayal, and it drove a wedge between us.
Between the business of planning an Indian wedding
and the stresses of a new job, we stopped talking as
much. By the time my wedding rolled around, which was
a mere two months later, she was just another guest in
the crowd.

The wedding was nothing like I had imagined. The
catered food was bad. The alcohol was overpriced. The
entire affair was way too extravagant for my liking.

On the morning of my wedding, Saira and my mom
were adjusting my lengha choli when my sister, looking
out at the venue, asked, "Jeez, how many people are

invited to this thing?" I rolled my eyes. "600." Her eyes opened wide in disbelief. No, I didn't know 600 people. Most of the guests were Arun's.

I tried to tell my mom that this wedding was not what I had always imagined. She hushed me. "Never mind all that. The important thing is that you're getting married." How I wished Veera would have been back there with me then. I never expected to be distant from her on my wedding day.

"I miss Veera," I finally said out loud, as my mother pinned the last of my dupatta to my head. "Well, now, it's time for you to focus on Arun. He is your family now." Not helpful.

I glanced over at Saira, and she gave me an air hug. And with that, I pushed myself through the wedding, reminding myself that this was the dream. I should be happy.

As the months went on, that dream started to crack. Arun wasn't the person I thought he was.

At first, it was little things—comments about my clothes, suggestions to "dress more modestly." Then, there was the criticism. I should take cooking lessons from his mother. I shouldn't drink in front of people for the sake of his image. My personality was... it was "too much." Slowly, he began to chip away at who I was, molding me into his idea of the perfect Indian wife:

quiet, obedient, invisible.

And that's how I started to feel. We had moved into his apartment in Alexandria, a fourth story loft with a nice view of the downtown. Everything was black and white. The furniture was modern. A black leather sectional looked great but was uncomfortable to sit on. It was all very...dry and colorless. I made a mental note to get colorful throws or paintings to brighten the space up.

As I unloaded my laundry one day, Saira called, her weekly check in.

"How's married life, sis?"

Trying, as always, not to give away how I was really feeling, I quickly diverted the conversation. It was always safer to ask the person on the other end questions than to talk about myself. I was afraid I would spill my true feelings if I was doing the talking.

"Oh, living the dream, you know. What's new with you?"

I kept it all inside. In our culture, you don't air your marital issues. To share your problems outside the home—that was a betrayal. To even admit there was a problem was to admit failure, and failure wasn't an option. So, I convinced myself that this was all just part of being married.

Before I knew it, it was time for our green card

interview. Like many Indian-Americans, Arun had come to the US as a child, but he wasn't a citizen. Marrying me meant he could apply for permanent residency in the country. I didn't think much about it, as this was such a common circumstance among Indian people in the US.

Despite my unhappiness, I gathered wedding photos, texts, and emails we had exchanged over the years, to show the immigration officer that this was anything but a sham marriage. Maybe the entire idea of marriage was a big sham, but not this. I stood by him proudly as his green card was approved. And that's when the unthinkable happened.

CHAPTER 18

KABHI KHUSHI, KABHI GONE

The late afternoon sunlight was soft and golden as I drove home from work. I had settled into my position in the public relations department at the Association for Advancing Electronics. Our job was to inform the public about trends in electronics and lobby for advancement. I researched and wrote articles on the latest advancements in technology. Every day was new and exciting.

I had just finished writing a piece on the newest features of a mechanical robot that would vacuum floors automatically. I should be excited to get home and share the details with Arun, but I knew the night would go nothing like that. Our nights were full of silence, despite

downtown Alexandria buzzing with activity just outside
our front door. My phone sat in the passenger seat,
and I hit the call button to check in with Arun. It went
straight to voicemail. Strange. Usually, he was home by
now, lounging in front of the TV or scrolling through his
phone. Maybe he was caught up at work.

The drive was familiar. The streets were lined with
charming brick buildings and boutique shops. On paper,
everything about my life looked perfect. A beautiful
loft apartment with a stunning view of downtown, a
blossoming career, and a marriage that, to outsiders,
seemed like a Bollywood movie come to life.

But the reality of my life with Arun was anything
but cinematic. Our days had settled into a dull, stifling
routine. I woke up each morning to make the bed,
prepare breakfast, and pack his lunch. The house was
spotless, the meals were made, and the laundry was
folded. And yet, I couldn't shake the feeling that I was
living someone else's life. Is this what I worked so hard
for? Is this why I got a degree and built a career? To live
like a servant in a gilded cage? Neglected?

Arun and I barely spoke anymore. The only words
exchanged were mundane, transactional: Did you pick
up the dry cleaning? Dinner was too salty. Why didn't
you vacuum today? His critiques had become a daily
routine, eroding my confidence bit by bit. And yet, I kept

                              The "I" in Indian

going, convincing myself that things would get better, that maybe I wasn't trying hard enough.

As I turned the corner to our street, something felt off. The loft was dark. Arun always beat me home. I climbed the stairs wearily. When I unlocked the door and stepped inside, a strange silence greeted me. No TV, no sound of his phone notifications pinging. Just... nothing.

"Arun?" I called out, setting my purse down on the counter. No response. My stomach twisted. Something was wrong.

The eeriness began to claw at me as I moved deeper into the apartment. That's when I noticed the empty space where the TV had been. My eyes darted to the shelves—bare. The stereo system was gone. The glass kitchen table, gone. My heart pounded in my chest as panic set in. I thought we had been robbed.

I reached for my phone to call the police, but then I stopped. Something inside me whispered that this wasn't a robbery. I turned toward the hallway, my legs heavy as I walked to our bedroom. The closet door was ajar, and I could already feel the answer before I looked. I slid the door open.

All of Arun's clothes were gone.

The room tilted, my stomach lurching as I scanned the rest of the apartment. His shoes, his cologne, his watch. All—gone. The realization hit me like a punch to the gut. He had left.

I sank onto the floor, staring at the empty space where his belongings used to be. The air felt thick, suffocating. My chest tightened as I tried to piece it together. The bank account. The green card. The critiques. Everything clicked into place. Arun had waited for his green card to be approved, and then he had just left. He had taken everything—electronics, appliances, even my jewelry. He didn't just leave me. He had wiped me out in the process.

Tears burned my eyes, but I couldn't cry. My body felt too numb, too stunned, to process what had just happened. Instead, I reached for my phone and dialed the only people I could think of—my parents.

My mother picked up on the second ring. "Aria? What's wrong?"

"He's gone, Ma," I said, my voice trembling. "Arun... he left. He took everything."

There was a pause. For a moment, I thought she might express shock, or anger, or (dare I hope) support. But when she finally spoke, her words cut deeper than I could have imagined.

"What did you do, Aria? How could you let this happen? You must fix this at once."

The tears I had held back now spilled over—but not

                    The "I" in Indian

for Arun. For me. For the weight of her disappointment. She didn't ask if I was okay. She just placed the blame squarely on my shoulders.

"Ma, I didn't...," I began, but she cut me off.

"This will bring shame to our family. Do you understand that? You can't just let him leave like this. You need to talk to him. Apologize if you must."

Apologize? The word echoed in my mind, my tears drying, as anger began to take its place.

"You think this is my fault?" I asked, my voice breaking. Desperately needing validation and knowing it wasn't coming.

Before my mother could respond, I heard a rustling sound on the other end, followed by my father's voice. He had taken the phone from her. Finally, surely, my father would be outraged. Arun had abandoned his daughter. He had stolen from her. Surely, my father would be on his way to kick his ass. He would be furious at Arun, disappointed in him.

Instead, his voice was calm, deliberate.

"Your mother is right," he said. "He is your husband. You are his responsibility now, and you two need to figure it out as a married couple."

I almost dropped the phone. The words didn't compute. It was like they were speaking a language I didn't understand. My father—the man I had spent my whole life seeking approval from—wasn't even angry. He wasn't outraged or disgusted by what Arun had done. He was simply handing me off like a transaction already completed. I was not his problem anymore.

Between my mother's judgment and my father's indifference, something inside me snapped. My stomach lurched with realization. I was truly alone in this. There was no home to run back to, no parental comfort to soften the blow. There was only me.

I gripped the phone tighter, my nails pressing into my palm. I had spent my whole life seeking their approval, molding myself into the perfect Indian daughter. And for what? When I needed them most, they turned away, leaving me to carry the weight of abandonment alone.

I didn't fail. Arun did. Arun failed me. And my parents had failed me, too. I straightened my back, wiping away my tears. If I was going to get through this, I would have to do it without them.

CHAPTER 19

AFTER THE FALL

My chest felt hollow, like everything inside me had collapsed under the weight of my parents' disappointment.

Arun had gutted me—emptied my life both literally and figuratively. And now, my parents—the one safety net I thought I could rely on—they weren't going to catch me.

I was completely untethered, floating in an unbearable void.

I picked up my phone again and dialed Veera's number. It had been months since we'd last spoken. I'd been too stubborn to hear her warnings. But now, as soon as I heard her voice, the dam broke.

"Aria?" she said, her tone immediately shifting to

concern.

I couldn't stop myself from sobbing into the phone. "He's gone, Veera. He left me, and he took everything with him."

There was a pause, but I could hear her sharp intake of breath. When she finally spoke, her voice was full of fire.

"Tell me where you are. I'm coming to get you."

Between sobs, I managed to fill her in, and Veera didn't waste a second.

"Pack whatever you can. I'll be there soon."

True to her word, Veera arrived at my door within an hour, her eyes blazing with anger. But her demeanor was calm and focused. Together, we boxed up what was left of my life. It didn't take long. Arun had already stripped it bare.

Still, Veera made sure I packed everything I might need: clothes, documents, down to the last stray bottle of shampoo.

"You're staying with me," she said firmly, as she hauled the last box into her car.

We arrived at her apartment in the next town over. I was barely able to see through my tears, but it was quintessential Veera—bright, eclectic, colorful, decorated with all sorts of plants and minimal furniture. The walls were adorned with mismatched art prints and colorful tapestries, and the air carried a faint smell of sandalwood incense. It was a space that felt alive, full of personality—the exact opposite of the sterile emptiness I was leaving behind.

"We'll share the couch," Veera said, motioning toward the oversized sectional covered in throw blankets. "It's cozy, and, honestly, better than the crappy bed I've got in my room. Make yourself at home."

I tried to thank her, but the words caught in my throat. Instead, I nodded, blinking back tears. The rest of the day was a blur. She tried to get me to eat, but I was sick to my stomach. For now, I just needed to exist.

The next morning, I called in sick. Too embarrassed to tell them what had really happened, I said I had a stomach bug. There was a knock on the door, and Veera went to answer it, surprised to have a visitor so early in the morning.

A man in a suit stood there, holding a brown envelope. "Is Aria Kapoor here?" She nodded and asked me to come to the door. Half-asleep, I shuffled to the door. "Yes?"

"You've been served," he said flatly, quickly handing me the envelope and leaving.

I stared at it for a moment, my stomach twisting. My hands trembled as I tore it open, pulling out the papers.

Divorce papers.

A flood of emotions hit me all at once.

First, there was confirmation. This had been planned, plotted. It was intentional. Divorce papers don't just appear out of nowhere a day after someone leaves. He'd been preparing for this—likely for weeks, maybe months.

Next came confusion. Why would he do this to me? Abandoning someone with no notice, no warning. That's what you do to an enemy, not someone you've known for years, someone you married.

"That fucking bastard," Veera exclaimed, slamming the door shut behind the server. "I knew he was no good. How convenient. He gets his green card approved and then pulls this? I could kill him!"

I tried to feel anger. To summon the fiery indignation I knew I deserved to feel.

But the embarrassment, the shame, and the sheer weight of rejection overpowered everything else.

And then the calls started.

The news spread like wildfire. It started with my mother and father. But, soon enough, my aunts, uncles, cousins, and even former dance team members were reaching out. Some were convinced I should take action with immigration. Others were hoping I would find a way to reconcile. All were shocked.

It didn't matter. I had made up my mind. I did not want to be married to someone who had it inside of themselves to abandon me without a word. I had every intention of following through with a divorce. So, I disappeared.

I ignored every call, deleted my social media profiles, and let myself vanish into silence. I just wanted to be alone. To heal.

For days, I barely left the couch, depleting all of my PTO. Days blurred into weeks, punctuated only by brief moments of forced interaction when I had to go back to work.

Veera sat beside me quietly, letting me process. Her presence was a silent reassurance that I wasn't alone. Her usual fire was absent. She didn't try to downplay my pain or tell me to snap out of it. She just stayed there, playing gatekeeper to anyone who wanted to interact with me. She never pushed me. She let me cry, scream, or sit in silence, offering gentle support without ever making me feel like a burden.

But I shut everyone else out, including Saira. She had been away at college when it happened, but she never stopped trying. She called every week, just to check on me. Most of the time, her calls went straight to voicemail. When I didn't answer, she kept in touch with Veera instead, sending her support from a distance.

Saira understood. She knew that, right now, I needed to lick my wounds. She knew I felt safe with Veera—protected from everyone who tried to make me feel bad. She knew that I would come back to her when I was ready.

As the dust settled and I had time and space to process what had happened, I started to feel more clarity about what to do. I had never believed in divorce, as my ideas of marriage were deeply wrapped up in Bollywood ideologies. I had always imagined that if I had issues in my marriage, I would persevere and push through. No issue could be too big; there could be no reason to give up. When we took vows, we vowed to lifetimes together, and I had meant it.

But there I was, standing corrected. There are, in fact, good reasons to get divorced. There are, in fact, things that are unforgivable, and this was one of them.

Saira, finally fed up with my distance, decided to pay us a visit for the weekend. The front door swung open. Saira, standing there, with a bright grin. She had cut her hair short and gotten highlights, which really brought out the olive in her skin. When she first saw me, she noticed how thin I looked, how tired. Without a word, she walked up to me and wrapped me in a long, reassuring hug. And just like that, we were okay.

"Get your shoes on, ladies," Veera exclaimed.

"Saira's visiting, and this calls for a trip to the Bad Rose!"

Letting go of our embrace, I smiled. That actually sounded kind of nice. Being out, getting lost in the music for a few hours. It sounded kind of nice. For the first time in months, I felt better, ready to get out and blow off some steam with some Patron shots and my girls.

Bad Rose was popular on Friday nights, and there was a line outside. Veera walked right up to the bouncer and cut the line, dragging us with her. "Dang, Veera." Saira was impressed. "You are popular around here!" Veera laughed, brushing her shoulders off, "Aria and I used to come here a lot—before she fell off the scene and into her enslavement." I smiled, not sure if I was ready to joke about it or not but appreciating Veera's attempt to make me laugh.

Veera led the charge, elbowing our path to the crowded bar. We secured a little nook away from the speaker, so that we could hear each other talk. After our third round of shots, Saira "Guess what?" she said, wiggling her eyebrows.

I stared at her blankly.

She rolled her eyes. "You're supposed to ask, 'What?'"

I sighed. "What?"

Veera shouted, "Are you pregnant!?"

Saira rolled her eyes at Veera. "I got into medical school!"

That caught my attention. I blinked. "Wait. What?"

She flopped onto the couch next to me, her excitement bubbling over. "Yep! I'm officially going to be a doctor. Woo!"

Despite my dark cloud of misery, I felt something break through. Pride.

I reached for the next shot and raised it like a toast.

"To **Doctor** Saira Kapoor! Cheers!"

She clinked her shot glass against mine. We linked arms and gulped the vodka down. I was going to regret this tomorrow.

But something about it nagged at me. I studied her carefully.

"Are you sure this is what you want?" I asked. "You're not doing this just because Mom and Dad think you should, right?"

She waved me off. "Stop. Don't worry."

Which wasn't really an answer. She wasn't lying... exactly. But she wasn't being completely honest, either.

Still, I let it go, because at that moment, it wasn't about me. It was about her. She had chosen a path, and she was running toward it full speed ahead. And even if I wasn't sure why she was running, I knew one thing for certain. I was proud of her.

We sat for a while, talking and catching up, until finally, a drunk Veera finally exclaimed, "I never liked Arun. He always gave me a bad vibe."

Saira added to that, "Yeah, the way he asked you to get married so quickly. I knew something wasn't right."

I stared at Saira, surprised, "Really? Why didn't you say anything?"

Veera answered for her. "As if you would have listened."

True. Definitely a lesson learned. I was curious, "So, how are Mom and Dad handling all of this?"

Saira sighed. "Well, at this point, we've all sort of accepted your decision to go through with the divorce. Sure, they have to deal with the whispers and questions from family members. But, Aria, they are also devastated for you."

I scoffed, shaking my head. "I doubt they're devastated for me. More like they are devastated for themselves."

Saira exhaled and reached for my hand. "Never mind all of that. Just focus on healing. They'll be there when you're ready to start coming out in public again. We all will."

I gave her a weak smile. "At least, they have you. One daughter is living up to what they want."

Saira didn't say anything. She didn't have to. We both knew it was true.

CHAPTER 20

BEHIND CLOSED CURTAINS

"Nothing romantic, please. I can't handle that right now," I said firmly, curling up on Veera's couch with my Gatorade clutched closely to my chest. My hangover was not allowing me to sit up straight. It was worth it, though. I danced until my feet hurt, laughed until my throat was coarse, and finally saw a glimmer of hope that I was going to be okay.

Veera rolled her eyes but didn't argue. "Fine, fine. No mushy Bollywood love stories. How about this one?" She held up the DVD case for Murder. Oooh, I had heard about this Indian movie. It was supposed to be thrilling. The title alone seemed promising. "Sounds perfect," I replied. "Popcorn ready?"

Veera tossed the bowl onto the sofa and plopped onto the couch beside me. The warm smell of salty popcorn was exactly what I needed right now. The opening credits rolled in, with a moody, mysterious soundtrack. Just what I needed. Veera and I had always bonded over our shared love for Bollywood movie nights, complete with commentary, snacks, and re-enactments of dance numbers. It was one of the few things that felt normal in my life, like a tether to the parts of me that hadn't been shattered by the divorce.

The movie kicked off with the stunning Mallika Sherawat, a woman who stepped up to marry her deceased sister's husband, so that her nieces and nephews would have a mother. She was trapped in a loveless marriage to a workaholic. After running into an old flame, she strikes up an affair with him. I noticed Veera shifting in her seat. She crossed and uncrossed her legs, her arms folded tightly across her chest.

I glanced at her, concerned. She usually had something witty to say about every scene. "You good?" I asked, but she just waved me off.

Her discomfort grew as the plot thickened. The popcorn bowl sat untouched between us. When Mallika's character leaned in for a particularly steamy scene, Veera shot up from the couch like it was on fire.

"Okay, that's it," she snapped, grabbing the remote

     The "I" in Indian

and hitting pause.

I blinked at her. "What is going on?"

"I don't want to watch this," she muttered, storming into the kitchen.

I followed her, my confusion growing with every step. "Veera, what's wrong? Do you not like the movie?"

She didn't answer right away. Instead, she yanked open the fridge and stared into it like it held the answers to the universe. Or maybe she was breathing in the cold air. Finally, she let out a heavy sigh, closing the fridge and leaning against the counter.

"It's not the movie," she said, her voice low.

I waited, giving her the space to continue. Veera wasn't one to open up easily. But, I could tell something was weighing heavily on her.

She glanced at me, her face uncharacteristically vulnerable. "Do you know why I hate Indian men so much?"

The question caught me off-guard. Veera's disdain for Indian men wasn't exactly a secret, but she'd never explained it, and I'd never pushed.

"No, why?" I asked gently.

She took a deep breath, as if summoning the courage to dive into something she'd buried for a long time.

"I was nine," she began, her voice trembling

slightly. "We were living in India, in Delhi. I typically played outside with my friends until dinnertime. But, on this particular day, I was feeling tired, so I went home early. My mom was out running errands, and my dad was supposed to be working. But when I walked into the house..." She trailed off, her jaw tightening.

"What happened?" I prompted softly.

"I found him," she said, her words laced with bitterness. "With my schoolmaster. They were in my parent's bed. I didn't even know what I was seeing at first, but, when I realized..." She shook her head, her eyes narrowing. "I was mortified. I ran out of the house and hid until I was sure the coast was clear. I waited for what must have been hours. It was nightfall by the time I returned home. My mother was worried sick, saying she had been out searching for me for hours. My father was asleep, unbothered. I told her everything. I thought she'd... I don't know...throw him out, wake him up, shake him, demand answers, something."

"And?" I asked, already dreading the answer.

Veera let out a bitter laugh. "She just looked at me, bending down and putting her hands on my shoulders, calm as ever, and said, 'Don't tell anyone. Pretend you didn't see anything." She slammed her hand against the counter for emphasis.

" 'It's important to keep a clean image in the

                    The "I" in Indian

community' she told me. That was it. Just swept it under the rug like it never happened. I was nine, Aria. Nine. And I was expected to carry that secret."

I stared at her, stunned. "She didn't do anything?"

"Nothing," Veera said, her voice sharp. "And my dad? He just carried on like nothing happened. To this day, he's the perfect dad, the perfect husband, in front of everyone. But I know the truth. And my mom? She just let it happen. She let him get away with it."

Her voice cracked, and she looked down, gripping the edge of the counter. "I wish she had set a better example for me," she said quietly. "If a woman can't respect herself, why would anyone else respect her?"

My heart ached for her, for the little girl who had been forced to shoulder something so heavy, so unfair.

"That's why I am the way I am," Veera continued, her voice regaining its usual edge. "That's why I don't give a flying fuck about what anyone thinks. Because at the end of the day, all Indian people care about is their image. Their precious reputation. And I can't live like that. I won't."

Her words struck a chord deep within me. Over time, she built up so much resentment toward her parents and had felt so alone. So, she had to carve her own path forward. Although my circumstances were different, I was in a similar situation. My own family cared more about the image of divorce than the necessity of it. My parents' disappointment in me wasn't about what I'd endured; it was about how it reflected on them.

I embraced her tightly, and she sobbed in my arms. She had been such a rock for me, and I wanted to be the same for her. I wanted to tell her, "It's OK. Sometimes, our parents make mistakes, and we can still love them." But I didn't really believe it in that moment myself, so I just held her and let her be sad.

After a few minutes, I pulled away from her and said, "You know what? Let's go somewhere."

Veera wiped her eyes. "Where?"

"Anywhere," I said. "We need to escape, get away. We need to reset, start over, and let go of all this pain."

She sniffled, then smirked. "Vegas?"

A slow grin spread across my face. "Vegas."

And that's how the tradition began.

I trace my finger over the edges of the photo, remembering Veera's laugh, her fearless energy, her unwavering sense of self, her courage to carve her own path. Years of having a friend like her had to rub off on

The "I" in Indian

me a little, right? I slip another photo into the album and glance at my mother. Her face is calm as she flips through photos in peace.

For an outsider looking in, we look so cute, sitting on the floor going through old photos together. But, the relationship is fake because I am still not living my truth. I am still living like some ashamed little girl. Can there be such a thing as a good relationship when you are hiding your true feelings? I need to embrace my inner "Veera-ness." Years of friendship with someone like her has to have taught me something, right? She had to rub off on me a little, right?

My mother doesn't see the storm brewing inside me. She doesn't know how hard I am working just to sit here, smiling, healed, and ready to try at love again, ready for a life in which I am the hero of my own story, in which I accept myself for who I am.

Suddenly, I feel ready to tell my mother what has been on my mind.

CHAPTER 21

LOVE, ACTUALLY
(HAS TERMS AND CONDITIONS)

"I want to talk to you, Mom," I say, my voice steady, but my heart pounding.

She pauses, a photograph still in her hand. "Alright. Let me finish putting these photos away, and we can chat."

"No, Ma," I interrupt. "This can't wait."

She looks up at me, her expression curious. "What's on your mind?"

I hesitate, gripping the edge of the chair in front of me. "Ma, I've been thinking a lot about...everything. About who I am, what I've been through, and how you've always seen me."

Her back stiffens, but a flicker of concern crosses

her eyes. "What are you talking about, Aria?"

"I want to talk about the divorce." The word hangs in the air between us, sharp and unyielding. I watch her expression shift—her lips tightening slightly, her eyes narrowing, the way they always do whenever the subject comes up.

"Why bring that up now?" she asks cautiously.

"Because I'm tired of pretending like I am ashamed of it, Ma. I'm tired of feeling like it defines me. And most of all, I'm tired of feeling like I've let you down because of it."

Her shoulders straighten, her defenses rising. "So, are you saying you are not ashamed of it, then?"

I feel my temperature rising, the rage bubbling inside me. "What exactly should I be ashamed of? The fact that Arun left me high and dry after getting a green card—or the fact that I didn't get down on my knees and beg to stay with someone like that?"

My mother listens, but her expression remains stern. "Aria, you know it's not that simple. You come from a good family, and we raised you to uphold certain values. Divorce... it's not something that is easily acceptable in our society."

I take a deep breath, summoning my courage. "That's exactly why I need to talk to you, Ma. Because we need to redefine what those values mean—what love means."

She blinks, caught off-guard. "Love?"

"Yes, Ma. Love. Because in our culture, love is about obedience. It's about doing your duty—obeying your parents, your husband, your in-laws. That's what you taught me. That's what I believed for a long time. But that's not love, Ma. At least, it is not for me."

She tilts her head, her brow furrowing. "Then, what is it to you?"

"Love is about compassion, fairness, and respect," I answer, my voice unwavering. "It's about seeing someone for who they are and supporting them—not trying to control them. Love isn't about sacrifice at the cost of your own happiness. It's about partnership, equality, and kindness."

She looks away, her hands fumbling with the edges of the photo. "Maybe in your Bollywood movies, but the reality is that marriage takes a lot more than love."

I stare back at her, confused but curious about what she thinks. She carries on, "Marriage also takes a lot of acceptance and forgiveness. It's not always singing in the fields and walking on the beach. It requires compromise and sacrifice."

I don't necessarily disagree with those things, but I push forward. "I don't disagree, but there are limits to that. A marriage isn't a free pass to treat someone however you want while the other person just has to deal with it. Love might be unconditional, but marriage has conditions—at least for me it does."

Her lips part, but no words come out. I can see the struggle in her eyes—the tension between the values she was raised with and the truth that I am laying bare.

"Ma, Arun did not love or respect me," I say, my voice cracking. "He hurt me. He controlled me, criticized me, used me for a green card, and left me. I thought being obedient and trying to live up to his standards would make me a good wife and happy. But it didn't make me a good wife, Ma; it made me miserable. I am glad he left."

She exhales, shaking her head. "You never think beyond yourself, Aria. You shut the whole world out. You hid away in your safe haven, while the rest of us had to deal with the community, the whispers, the mocking, the jokes."

I feel a pang of frustration. "Because you blamed me, Ma! You were and are still more worried about what the world would think than how I felt. And this community you are so worried about...have you thought about what kind of community this really is? Something awful happens to one of their own, and, instead of offering support, sympathy, or compassion, they offer only judgement and shame."

I take a breath, steadying myself. "I needed to go through those things to become who I am today. So, no, I don't have the same definition of love as you do. I don't see it as obedience. I see it as a choice."

Her eyes glisten, and I know she feels the weight of my words. She lets out a big sigh. She is hearing me—finally. But, I can see a sense of defeat on her face. "These traditions have been around for generations, Aria. They're not easy to let go of."

"If you guys can't even accept my divorce, how can I expect someone new to accept it?" I ask, my voice quiet but firm. For a fleeting moment, I consider the possibility of telling her about Leo. Maybe, just maybe, I could open that door.

She sighs, wiping away her tears. "Even if we accept it, Aria, that doesn't mean the outside world will."

The moment passes. The door closes. It still isn't time to bring up Leo.

I stare at her, absorbing her words.

"Even if we can understand," she continues, "that doesn't mean the whole world will. And you do ultimately have to live in this world, in this society. You do have to care a little bit about what people think."

She takes a breath. For the first time, her voice is softer, more vulnerable. "I am sorry, Aria. I am not ashamed that you are divorced. But I am also who I am.

These are my beliefs, my traditions, my worries. They are not easy to change."

I nod slowly, a mutual understanding forming between us. Maybe we would never fully agree. But at least I now know that she is not ashamed of me. And that, for today, is enough.

For the first time in years, I feel a weight lift from my shoulders. My mother's acknowledgment, her willingness to meet me halfway, is the liberation I hadn't realized I had been searching for.

I hug her tightly, tears streaming down both our faces. "I love you, Aria," she whispers between tears. In that moment, I finally feel whole—because, for the first time, I am strong enough to demand the love I deserve—from her, from the world, and most importantly, from myself.

CHAPTER 22
ADRIFT

It's been two weeks since Aria stormed out of our hotel room. Other than a short text, I haven't heard from her since. I replay that night over and over again in my head, trying to figure out what the hell happened. One moment, I am standing on the beach, proud and vulnerable, hoping my grand gesture would make her feel cherished. The next, she is gone, leaving me alone in a hotel room, staring down from the balcony at the high tide erasing the last vestiges of my declaration of love. I have never felt so helpless—or so confused.

I don't know what I did wrong. Was it the timing? Was it too soon to say I loved her? Did I misread everything about us?

Sitting on the porch of my parents' house, I stare out at the sprawling green lawn, freshly cut and soaked in golden sunlight. Dad is in his favorite rocking chair, sipping on a scotch while reading the paper. My mom is somewhere inside, baking cookies for the neighborhood kids. It's a picturesque, peaceful day. But all I can think about is Aria.

"Want to talk about it?" Dad's voice breaks the silence, pulling me out of my thoughts.

I glance over at him, unsure of where to start. My dad isn't the type to pry, but he has this uncanny ability to know exactly when something's weighing on me. "It's complicated," I finally say, leaning back in my chair.

"Women usually are," he replies with a chuckle. He folds the newspaper and sets it on the small table beside him, giving me his full attention. "But complicated doesn't mean impossible. What happened?"

I take a deep breath. "I told her I love her."

He raises an eyebrow. "That's a bad thing?"

"I don't know. I thought it was the right time. Things had been going so well between us. I wanted her to know how I felt, but... she didn't exactly take it well." I pause, staring out at the horizon.

"She told me she's divorced."

Dad doesn't react immediately, letting the weight of my words settle between us. When he finally speaks, his tone is calm and steady. "And how do you feel about that?"

"I don't know," I admit. "I didn't see it coming. She was so upset when she told me—like she expected me to judge

                    The "I" in Indian

her or to leave. But I wasn't upset because she's divorced. I was upset because she didn't trust me enough to tell me sooner. It felt like she was running away before I even had a chance to process it."

Dad nods thoughtfully. "People carry baggage, son—some more visible than others. The question isn't whether she has baggage; it's whether you're willing to carry it with her."

I consider his words, thinking back to the time I've spent with Aria. Her laugh, her smile, the way she lights up when she talks about her passions. The way she looked at me that night on the beach, torn between wanting to stay and wanting to run.

"I don't care that she's divorced," I finally say. "I care about her. But she has to let me in."

Dad leans back in his chair, a satisfied look on his face. "Then you need to let her know that. And you need to be patient. Sometimes, people don't share their pain because they're ashamed of it. You've got to make it clear that you're not going anywhere, no matter what."

I nod, feeling a flicker of hope. He's right. If I want a future with Aria, I need to show her that I'm here to stay—not just for the easy moments, but for the hard ones, too.

"Thanks, Dad," I say, standing up and stretching.

He waves me off with a grin. "Don't thank me yet. I expect to see her again soon, so we can share a glass of scotch, and she can tell us about her life."

I laugh, feeling a little lighter for the first time in days. As I head to my car, I pull out my phone and scroll through my contacts. I hesitate for a moment before pressing Aria's name.

The phone rings once, twice, three times. For a moment, I think it's going to go to voicemail. But then, I hear her voice.

"Hello?"

My heart races at the sound. "Hey, Aria. It's me. Can we talk?"

There's a long pause. I can hear the hesitation in her silence. But finally, she responds, her voice soft and cautious.

"Okay."

It's a start.

CHAPTER 23

BAGGAGE CLAIM ACCEPTED

In the few days that followed the conversation with my mom, it was like a weight had been lifted off my chest. I put on a white maxi dress with cutouts near the stomach and decorated with bright, bold, blue flowers. Matching white strappy sandals, of course. For the first time in years, I feel as though I can truly breathe. I still need to face my dad, but that is a problem for another day. For now, I feel like running to the person who deserves the best, most honest version of me: Leo. Getting a call from him was surprising. I didn't think he would ever talk to me again after the way I left him. But, hearing his deep voice was all it took to bring me right back to how I felt about him weeks ago.

I stared at his name on my phone, I'm sitting on a bench now, feeling equally nervous and determined. I am ready to tell him my story and deal with the reaction. I want him to know me, all of me—the good, the bad, and everything in between. No more self-sabotage, no more doubting my worth. I am finally ready to be vulnerable.

I asked him to meet me at the Lindin Plaza, a happening place lined with restaurants that all surround a public space filled with waterfalls, live music events, and comfortable benches. It's Saturday, so the place is alive with kids running around, dogs barking, and the faint strum of a street performer's guitar. When I walk up, Leo is already there, sitting on a bench under one of the trees. His eyes light up the moment he sees me, and I feel my chest tighten with a mix of hope and anxiety.

"Hey," he greets me, standing up as I approach. His eyes are a deeper blue than I remember, and his dimples taunt me. He's such a sight for sore eyes.

"Hi," I reply, smiling nervously.

We sit down, and, for a few moments, we just watch the world go by. He doesn't press me, does not rush me to start talking, and I appreciate that. I appreciate him. Finally, I turn to him, meeting his patient, blue-eyed gaze.

"Leo, I'm sorry for running off the way I did. I am

                    The "I" in Indian

not proud of that. It was a classic case of self-sabotage," I
begin, tucking a stray strand of hair behind my ear.

His expression doesn't falter. He is totally and
completely focused on me.

"Okay," he says simply.

"I've been carrying something around with me for a
long time," I continue. "Something I have let define me
in ways it shouldn't have. And I realized that if I want
this—I mean, us—to work, I need to be honest with
you."

He nods, his eyes soft and attentive, encouraging
me to keep going.

"I was married before," I say, the words tumbling
out more easily than I ever would have expected.
"When I was 22. It happened fast, and I didn't see the
signs. My ex—Arun—he wasn't a good man. He used
me to get a green card. As soon as he got it, he left. He
took everything. Our bank account, our belongings...
everything. He even filed for divorce himself."

I pause, gauging his reaction, but his face remains
calm, though his jaw tightens slightly.

"I spent years feeling like I had failed—like I wasn't
good enough. My culture...it made it worse. Divorce
is not exactly something to be proud of in my culture.
And, for a long time, I believed that I should be ashamed
of my situation. But I am not. What happened to me

doesn't define me. It is just part of my story. And I want to share all of my story with you—because you deserve that."

He looks up. The intensity in his eyes startles me.

"Why did you run off like that, Aria?" He looks defeated. "Why didn't you just tell me?"

"Because..." I try to find the words to explain this well. "I was raised to believe that being divorced is a deal-breaker, something like a scarlet letter. And I like you so much that I didn't want to ruin it—even though I kinda did."

The silence that follows feels heavy, heavier than I could have imagined. Leo's gaze drops to the ground, his brows furrowed in thought.

I realize I am holding my breath. I let it out.

"Say something," I finally whisper, my voice trembling slightly.

"I'm furious," he says, his voice low but steady.

I blink. "At me?"

"God, no," he says, shaking his head. "At him. At anyone who has ever made you feel like you're anything less than incredible. Aria, what he did to you—it's unforgivable. And the fact that you survived that and came out on the other side even stronger? That's... I don't even have words for how much I admire you."

Tears well up in my eyes, and I let out a shaky laugh.

          The "I" in Indian

"You're not mad at me?"

"Mad at you?" he repeats, scoffing. "Aria, I love you. I love everything about you—your strength, your fire, your honesty. And, if anything, knowing what you've been through just makes me want to love you harder. To prove to you every single day that you deserve the world."

I can't stop the tears from spilling over. "I was so scared you'd see me differently," I admit.

He reaches for my hand, pulls me closer until our foreheads touch. "The only thing I see," he murmurs into my hair, "is the woman I want to be with."

I close my eyes, letting his words sink in. For the first time, I feel completely seen. Completely accepted.

"I love you," I whisper, the words spilling out before I could second-guess them.

He pulls back, just enough to look me in the eyes, a wide smile spreading across his face. "I love you, too," he says. "So much."

The kiss that follows is soft and sweet, filled with all the words we didn't need to say. When we finally pull apart, he grins down at me.

"Now that we've got that out of the way," he says playfully, "what do you say we grab some ice cream? My treat."

I laugh, wiping my tears. "You know how to win a

girl over."

As we walk hand in hand toward the ice cream stand, I feel lighter than I have in years. I have faced my past, owned my truth, and found someone who loves me for every part of it.

And for the first time, I truly believe I deserve it.

CHAPTER 24

HALFWAY TO SHORE

I've never been in a relationship that feels this easy—this effortless. I watch Aria bounce around her kitchen, looking natural, happy. Aria and I have slipped into a rhythm that feels like we have been doing it for years. I can't even remember the last time I spent the night at my own place.

As she slips the baking tray into the oven, she looks at me, mischievous and excited, like she's made a masterpiece she can't wait for me to taste. "Don't get too excited now," I tease. "My expectations for Italian food are really high." I really am just teasing, though. The fact that she is trying to cook my favorite Italian stuffed shells from scratch for me is a simple thing, but it matters. No one has ever cared for me like this before. I am going to devour the food and then her.

I know, deep in my bones, that she is the one. I had never felt this kind of certainty before. I can feel it in every touch, every lingering glance, every time she reaches for my hand just because. We are crazy about each other.

But something is holding her back. Despite becoming my designated date for family dinners and work events, she is resisting introducing me to her parents. She has never said it outright, but I can feel it—that invisible line she isn't ready to cross.

I tell myself it makes sense. She has been through a lot. She will be careful about getting married again, about trusting someone with that part of her life. But I also want to keep this moving forward, so I am not ready to stop asking just yet. I just have to be patient and persistent. She will get there.

I finally get the courage to ask, "So, how about this weekend? Can we get together with Saira?" She pauses, her back turned away from me, and just stands there for a moment. She turns her head to the side of her shoulder, not making eye contact with me, and lets out a simple "okay."

Progress.

CHAPTER 25

EMOTIONAL TRIAGE

The phone rings twice before Saira picks up.

"Ugh. I'm horizontal. I'm not moving again until tomorrow," she groans by way of greeting.

I smile, relieved just to hear her voice. "Long shift?"

"The longest." Her voice is raw, and there's a weight to it I recognize too well. "Lost a girl today. Nineteen. I had to tell her parents... tell them she wouldn't make it through the night."

My heart catches. "Saira..."

"I'm okay. Or, I will be. I'm just..." she trails off, and I can hear the rustle of fabric as she pulls a blanket over herself. "I need a bath. And a good book. Something happy. Something where no one dies."

I sit with the silence for a beat, not wanting to crowd her grief. "Well, I have two pieces of good news. You get to see me tomorrow, and then it's Veera's wedding!"

She exhales a soft laugh. "God, yes. I've worked seven days straight to get the time off. I need that more than oxygen. I am going stay at Mom and Dad's so I can get my Indian clothes together, but I will meet you tomorrow for dinner."

We fall into a familiar rhythm of quiet catching up, her venting about the hospital politics, me rambling about a difficult client. The normalcy is comforting.

But I didn't call just to chat.

"There's one more thing," I say, trying to sound casual.

Saira hums in response. I can practically see her eyes closing, her body relaxing for the first time in hours.

"I want you to meet someone."

Her silence is instant and deafening. I push through it.

"Leo."

Now she shifts. I hear it. The small intake of breath. "You're ready for that?"

"I think I am." I bite my lip and then add, "I think things are getting serious."

She doesn't respond. I keep going.

"I know you're tired, and I know you probably want to give me a lecture or say you're not ready to meet anyone, but before you do..." I pause. "You told me to accept myself. This is part of that. I'm done hiding, Saira. I like him. He makes me feel like I'm enough. Like I don't have to be anyone else."

She lets out a sigh, long and heavy. I wait for her to talk me out of it, to tell me to slow down, or to be careful and not get hurt again.

But instead, she says, quietly, "You're lucky."

I blink. "What?"

"I spent all day watching a family lose a loved one, and I'm feeling exceptionally grateful that we all still have each other." Her voice cracks, just barely. "So yeah. I'll meet him."

I exhale, relief flooding through me.

"But," she adds, her voice sharp with mock warning, "only if you take me somewhere fun."

I laugh. "Deal."

"And I promise I'll be nice," she says, her tone softening again. "He clearly means something to you, because I know asking me this wasn't easy. Let's see what the hype is all about."

My eyes sting. "Thank you."

CHAPTER 26

ANCHORS AND ALIBIS

I get to the Oak & Vine wine bar early, showing up 10 minutes before our reservation to make sure everything is set up correctly. Oak & Vine is exceptionally busy today, which is not a surprise considering it is 80 degrees outside. The restaurant is known for serving some of the best butter chicken in town, and you don't see that on a bar menu often, so I am curious to try it.

I am not nervous about meeting Saira—not exactly—but I know how important it is. Aria and Saira communicate via Facetime, text, and memes every day. Aria has resisted this for weeks, always dodging the subject whenever I bring it up, always finding some excuse. But here we are. Finally, I am meeting someone in her family.

The restaurant is unique, one building on each side of a terrace, each with large garage doors opening up to the middle. Both buildings are their own bar but part of the same place. I pick a table in the center of the terrace, just far enough from the speakers so we can actually hear each other. The warm air moves through the open garage doors, carrying the soft strumming of a live guitarist playing some acoustic cover of a pop song. Perfect.

The rosé sits chilling in an ice bucket when I spot them walking toward me. Aria looks gorgeous as always, but I focus instead on her sister, on Saira.

She is taller than I expected, with thick, dark hair like Aria's but cut shorter, framing her sharp features. She walks with a kind of quiet confidence, but there is something soft around the edges, something open. Aria has described her as the golden child, the one who never rocks the boat. I wonder if that is actually true.

I stand as they reach the table. "Finally," I say, flashing a grin. "Saira, it's great to meet you."

She smirks as we shake hands. "Likewise. Aria's told me all about you."

I turn to Aria, arching a brow. "All good things, I hope?"

Aria rolls her eyes, but I catch the tiny smile before she sits down.

Saira glances at the open bottle of wine and then back at me. "Rosé, huh? Trying to win me over?"

I grin, pouring us each a glass. "I did my research. And I figure, if you like me, maybe you'll put in a good word for me with your parents."

That's when it happens. The flicker of something between them. A split-second glance exchanged between sisters, so fast I almost miss it. Almost.

I chuckle, but the feeling lodges in my chest. "That bad, huh?"

Saira swirls her wine. "Not bad. Just... complicated."

Aria looks down at her glass, silent.

I don't push. Instead, I turn to Saira, steering the conversation toward safer ground. I ask her about her medical program, what she does outside of work—though I suspect she doesn't have much time for that. She responds with enthusiasm. Bubbly, even.

She tells me about her most exhausting shifts, about patients who have surprised her, about how she and Aria used to make up fake diagnoses as kids, pretending to be doctors. She laughs easily, eyes bright, hands animated as she speaks.

I like her.

The conversation then shifts to her love life. Aria teases her about the latest string of dates she has been on—all arranged by her parents. "Oh, God. It's like one bad egg after another," Saira complains as she takes a sip of her wine.

As I listen, something else settles into place. For all of her confidence, for all of her warmth, she is careful. I can tell. She is someone who follows the rules—or at least, her parents' rules. She has never gone against them, not really.

Aria teases, "You can always come over to the bright side," nudging toward me, implying that her sister could try dating someone outside their culture. To which, Saira's eyes widen as she shakes her head no. "Yeah, right, like that would go over well," she responds, glancing over at me, quickly realizing that maybe she shouldn't have said that.

And that tells me everything I need to know.

Aria isn't just afraid her parents won't accept me. She knows they won't.

Saira, the golden child, the rule-follower, isn't saying, "It will be fine. You'll win them over. Just give it some time." No, she is not saying anything like that. So, what chance do I really have?

Saira changes the subject first.

"So, Leo," she says, tilting her head, clearly feeling the rosé a bit too much, "what are your intentions with my sister?"

Aria groans. "Oh, my God."

I don't even hesitate. "I'm serious about her. Very serious."

Saira studies me for a second, then gives a small nod. "Good answer."

I see Aria glance at me then, something unreadable in

                              The "I" in Indian

her expression. Before I can make sense of it, she stands. "I'm running to the bathroom."

She disappears inside, leaving me and Saira alone.

A brief pause.

I want to ask her more about her parents, but I think it might be better to stay on safe topics for the first meeting.

I clear my throat, reaching for my glass. "So... Veera's wedding... huh?"

Saira lights up. "Yup! Aria and I are road-tripping tomorrow. It's going to be amazing."

I smile. "Sounds great. I wish I could go. I hear it's a small wedding, though."

Saira doesn't hesitate. "Oh, no. She can have a plus one," she says, waving a hand. "Veera's her absolute best friend. She'd let Aria bring a homeless person if she wanted to. Aria has free rein at this wedding."

The words land hard.

I am not angry. I did not expect to be invited. But I realize something right then and there. Aria didn't invite me. I feel the shift inside me before I even register it. That slow, sinking understanding that, no matter what I do, no matter what I prove, the fact that I am not Indian will always be a problem.

Saira sees it on my face. She opens her mouth like she wants to fix it, but it is too late.

Aria comes back, slides into her seat, oblivious to the

moment she just missed. I smile at her, but something has most definitely shifted.

On the drive home, I can't shake it.

It all makes sense now.

The hesitation. The deflections. The way she pushed off meeting her family. The fact that she has never—not once—talked about introducing me to her parents.

I had told myself it was about timing. That she wasn't ready yet. That she needed space.

But what if it isn't about timing at all?

What if she is never going to be ready?

I tighten my grip on the steering wheel. I love her, all the way to my bones.

But love isn't enough.

I need acceptance. Not just in private, in stolen moments. I need to know that she will stand by me, out in the open—that Aria will fight for us.

And if she can't do that? Then I need to know that. Now.

# CHAPTER 27

IT'S NOT YOU, IT'S MY GENERATIONAL CONDITIONING

I stand there, staring at the colossal mess I have made while packing for Veera's wedding. Checking, double-checking, triple-checking that I have not forgotten anything.

Indian outfits are not just a piece of clothing. They are an entire ensemble—complete with matching bangles, bindis, tikkas, earrings, shoes, and a clutch. It's the ensembles that make Indian weddings so glamorous. Small weddings are unheard of in Indian culture. Typically, a full week-long affair, complete with seven different events, you need a different ensemble for each one. Veera's would only have two events. This is unheard of, so I keep feeling like I am forgetting something.

Glancing down at the clock, I see that is already noon. I know Saira will be here any minute, rushing me out the door. I just trust my multiple checks and get on with stuffing everything into my suitcase. As I am folding the last of my outfits into my suitcase, I hear the soft creak of my bedroom door.

"Hey." Leo's voice is warm. He hands me a to-go mug full of tea. He had spent the night with me, holding me extra tight. This will be the first time we are be apart in weeks, and I am going to miss him. I close my eyes and go in for a kiss, but he moves back. Something is off.

I open my eyes to see him leaning against the doorframe, his hands in his pockets, eyes scanning my half-packed bag. His gaze flicks to the vibrant fabrics spread across my bed—rich jewel-toned lehengas, embroidered kurtas, shimmering dupattas.

"Wow, those are really beautiful," he says. He's never seen them before, never seen me in them. I can tell by the look on his face that it pains him.

"Hey," I say softly. "Are you okay?"

He hesitates. A breath. A shift of weight from one

foot to the other.

I straighten. Something is wrong.

He exhales sharply, stepping into the room. "No, I don't think I am."

That surprises me. Leo is always composed, always the one grounding me. I finish zipping up the suitcase and stand up straight, my pulse quickening.

"Talk to me," I say, taking a step closer to him.

He runs a hand through his hair, looking at me like he is trying to figure out where to start. And then he just says it.

"Why didn't you invite me to the wedding, Aria?"

The air in the room shifts instantly. My stomach clenches.

I open my mouth, but he holds up a hand. "Before you say anything: I know you can easily get a plus one." His voice isn't angry, but it is firm. Certain. "Saira made that pretty clear the other day."

I swallow hard.

"I don't want to come off as clingy or needy," he continues. "I understand you have been through a lot, and I am trying to give you time and space. We've only been together a few months. But this? This isn't just about the wedding. This is about us. If we're going to be together, really together, I need you to be honest with me."

My chest tightens. I feel cornered, like there is nowhere to escape.

I open my mouth, hesitate, then finally admit the truth.

"I didn't invite you because I don't want my parents to find out."

Leo stares at me. "Why?"

"Because they won't..." I stop, struggling to find the right words. Words that won't make me sound weak. "Because I don't know how they will react."

He steps closer, his eyes searching mine. "Aria, it's one thing to not have me meet them. But are you telling me they don't know about me at all?"

I look down at the ground, unable to make eye contact, feeling ashamed that I didn't consider how that fact might make him feel.

Leo steps back, surprised, "You're in your 30s. You have your own place, your own career. You have been married and divorced. Do you parents seriously think you just—what?—don't date?"

I swallow. "It's not that simple." I swallow again. "Girls don't really 'date' in our culture. You only date someone if you're going to marry them."

He looks at me expectantly. "Okay, so what's the problem?" His look makes it clear that he does, in fact, have that intention. "Explain it to me." His voice is

     The "I" in Indian

steady, but I can hear the emotion pulsing beneath it. "Because from where I'm standing, I've given you full acceptance, Aria, and I have made my feelings pretty clear. I don't hide you from my life. I don't hesitate to tell people about us. And I want the same in return."

I close my eyes for a second, willing myself to keep it together.

"I do accept you," I whisper. "I do."

"But?"

I look up at him, and the answer finally slips past my lips.

"But I don't know if my parents will."

A silence stretches between us.

Then, Leo lets out a short, humorless laugh. "Why not?" he asks, shaking his head. "Is it because I am a teacher?"

I look back at him confused. Clearly, he has an insecurity that I missed. "No, of course not. I don't care about that. I have my own money," I say, convincingly.

"Then why? Why wouldn't they accept me? What is it about me that's so unacceptable to your parents?"

I feel myself shrink, because I know the answer.

And I hate it.

I take a breath—a shaky, fragile breath.

"Because you're not Indian," I say finally.

The words land like a slap.

Leo let them sit in the air for a moment, his
expression unreadable. Then, he takes a slow step back.

"Aria," he says, his voice measured, careful. "That's
racist."

I blink. Racist?

That word, coming from a white man, rattles me. I
have never thought of it that way before. In my family,
it has always just been expected that we would be with
someone from our own culture. That's how things work.
That's how they have always worked.

But Leo is right. Isn't it racist to say that someone
can't be accepted because of their race or culture? I feel
my stomach churn, a deep discomfort settling in my
chest.

Leo exhales and looks at me with something almost
like sadness. "I love who I am, Aria. I love my family,
my traditions, my background. And I love that you love
yours. But if your parents won't accept me just because
I'm not Indian, what does that mean for us?"

I stare at him, feeling like the walls of the room are
closing in.

He is asking me something serious. Something I
don't have an answer for. He isn't breaking up with
me—at least, not yet.

"If you don't think your parents can accept me," he
asks quietly, "then, what are we doing here?"

I open my mouth...

And we are interrupted.

"Aria, let's go!" Saira's voice rings out from the doorway. "We need to get on the road before traffic gets bad!"

A thick tension fills the space between the two of us. I have no idea what I was about to say.

And now? I have to leave. I have time to think about it.

CHAPTER 28

DANCING THROUGH THE DOUBT

Leo gives me a kiss on the cheek after loading my suitcase into the trunk of Saira's Jeep SUV. I can see the sadness in his eyes, but he doesn't show it to my sister.

He waves me off. As we drive off, I stare at him in the side-view mirror. I feel like crying. Despite everything I have put him through, he is still nice to me, loyal. The ache in my stomach feels like it is the size of Texas— heavy, impossible to ignore. He did not push for an answer, hadn't made any final decisions, but his words echoed in my head. "If you don't think your parents can accept me, then what are we doing here?"

I don't know.

Sensing my distraction, Saira tries to lighten the mood by striking up conversation.

"I am so excited that Veera is getting married!" she says enthusiastically. "Is this what you had imagined for her wedding day?"

I thought back to the many nights Veera and I spent watching grand weddings in Bollywood movies— imagining our own: the groom making a grand entrance on a white horse; synchronized dances to our favorite songs and a multi-day celebration full of music, food, and celebration.

"Not really, actually," I say. "Veera always talked about having the big bang Bollywood wedding. But, I guess your priorities just change as you grow up."

"Interesting," Saira adds. "But, it's still super exciting that she is getting married. I guess all that matters is that she is happy, right?"

I stare out the car window as Saira drives, my fingers twisting in my lap. The silence stretches between us as we hit the interstate. Then, out of nowhere, Saira says, "I like him, you know."

I turn to look at her, surprised. "Leo?"

She nods, eyes still on the road. "He's a good guy."

I want to ask her what I should do—if she thinks I could ever stand up to our parents and live life on my

                    The "I" in Indian

terms the way Veera has. But my mind is scattered, tangled up in too many emotions. And this isn't about me. This is Veera's weekend, and I am not going to let my problems overshadow it.

Veera and I had been best friends for more than a decade. We have stuck together through relationships, breakups, family drama, everything. Her parents won't even be there for her big day. We are her family.

For the next two days, I need to push everything else aside and be present for her.

That night, Saira and I get dressed in our lehngas (traditional embroidered skirts) We pair them with intricate crop tops and draping dupattas. Mine is deep maroon with gold embroidery, heavy with sequins that shimmer under the light. I line my wrists with matching bangles and clip a delicate tikka to my forehead, its gold chain resting in the part of my hair.

Indian weddings are their own kind of magic. The colors, the fabrics, the jewelry—it is a sensory overload in the best way. It makes you feel like royalty.

Veera's wedding would have only two functions: the Lady Sangeet and the wedding. Tonight is the Lady

Sangeet, my favorite wedding tradition. On this night, women gather, dressed to the nines, to sing old folk songs to the bride—teasing her about her future married life, showering her with love, and dancing until our feet give out.

The venue is a small ballroom in a random hotel, but it is decorated in bright, colorful silk drapes hanging from the chandeliers. Floral garlands cascade from archways, and twinkling lights cast a golden glow over the room. The whole space pulses with warmth and celebration.

My eyes immediately scan the room and find Veera. She looks absolutely stunning. A fiery orange lehnga-choli hugs her frame, sequined and embroidered with delicate threadwork. Her hair is pulled back into a sleek bun, woven with fresh jasmine flowers, traditional yet entirely her own.

The second she sees us, she grabs my arm and drags Saira and me straight to the bathroom.

"I haven't eaten a carb in two weeks just to fit into this outfit, and I am literally starving."

Before I can react, she pulls a samosa from under her dupatta and stuffs it into her mouth like she has just been freed from prison.

I burst out laughing. Of course.

Then she turns to me, mid-chew, and narrows her

eyes.

"What's wrong with you?" she demands. "I can see it all over your face."

Busted.

I force a smile. "Nothing's wrong! Now, let's go dance!"

She eyes me for another second, but I am not giving her more than that. Not tonight.

This is her moment.

The party is small—fewer than 30 people—but it doesn't matter.

Saira cannot contain herself. "Okay, I have to know everything about your husband-to-be. Spill!"

Veera grins. "Met him at a music festival. And no, the fact that he's Indian has nothing to do with why I'm marrying him. I would've picked him no matter what. He loves me. Respects me. Makes me laugh until I can't breathe. The fact that he understands our culture? That's just a bonus. And, honestly," she twirls once, showing off her lehnga, "I just like getting to dress up like a fairy-tale princess."

I laugh, but my stomach twists.

Saira beams. "That makes him a winner in my book."

I stare at her.

The same sister—the one who has always been so obedient, so scared of rocking the boat—she is suddenly saying exactly what I need to hear.

Does she not see the irony?

I have always assumed Saira would follow my parents' rules until the end of time. But tonight, she is genuinely happy for Veera—for choosing someone for love and not tradition.

And yet, I am not brave enough to do the same.

The rest of the night is pure joy.

Veera and I dance until our feet hurt, breaking out old routines from college, twirling, laughing, completely in our element.

At one point, we even put on a full Bollywood-style performance for her fiancé, reliving the ridiculous choreographed dances we used to do in our apartment when we pretended we were Bollywood movie stars.

When the song ends, we collapse into each other, breathless. Veera squeezes my hand, her eyes shining.

She has found her person.

I hug her tightly. "I'm so happy for you."

And I mean it.

The night eventually winds down. I go back to my room, kick off my heels, and crawl into bed. Inevitably, my thoughts drift back to Leo. His carefreeness. His kindness. The way he always dotes on me. I imagine him there on the dance floor, watching me, smiling.

I miss him.

I have found my person, too. But, unlike Veera, I have not been brave enough to stand by him.

Not yet.

I close my eyes, exhaustion pulling me under. Tomorrow is the wedding.

And after that?

I have a decision to make.

CHAPTER 29

AFTER PARTY

The garden in front of the temple is beautifully manicured. Boxwoods trimmed in perfect rectangles line the path to the oversized wooden doors that take you into a temple made entirely of white marble.

The three of us—Veera, Saira, and I—hide on the tiny balcony off the bridal suite on the top floor, pressed against the intricately carved railings and giggling like schoolgirls as we spy on the procession below. The guests cannot see us, but we can see everything.

The baraat, also known as the groom's grand entrance, is underway The groom arrives, his friends and family dancing with abandon. It is sheer joy. It is his moment to declare, loudly and proudly, that he is here to claim his bride.

He is not on a horse, which, honestly, is a relief.
No one needs an animal-related catastrophe on their
wedding day. But he is in the thick of it, dancing wildly,
surrounded by his friends and family, the drums beating
so hard I can feel them in my chest. He looks like a man
who cannot wait to marry the love of his life.

Veera's eyes fill with tears.

I turn to her immediately. "No, no, no!" I whisper
urgently. "We did not spend hours on your makeup for
you to ruin it now. And your mascara is not waterproof!"

She sniffles, waving me off. "I know, I know. I just...
Look at him."

I look. I see pure love.

The temple is breathtaking.

The white stone gleams in the sunlight, giving
the space a serene, almost otherworldly glow. Life-
sized sculptures of the deities stand tall, their peaceful
expressions watching over the ceremony. The
decorations are simple: deep red roses against the white
stone, a striking contrast that make everything feel
timeless.

Inside, the altar—a circular mandap surrounding a

                        The "I" in Indian

fire—is set. The sacred flames flicker between the two people starting on a new journey and who are now the heart of this ceremony. Veera holds my hand tightly as I walk her down the aisle to an eager fiancé. Her steps are slow, as if she is taking in every moment, remembering the long path to this very moment. I choke back my tears as I imagine what she must be feeling. As I hand her off to her fiancé, she squeezes my hand and looks at me, an unspoken exchange between us, in which she is asking me one last time. I nod, encouraging her to take the last steps up to the mandap. Then, I let go of her hand, placing it into his.

The saat phere, the seven sacred circles around the fire, are about to begin. Each step, each vow, is steeped in meaning:

First phera. We pray for nourishment and a good life.

Second phera. The groom promises to support his wife.

Third phera. We pray for wealth and prosperity.

Fourth phera. We pray for love, trust, and respect.

Fifth phera. We promise to care for our loved ones and nurture our home.

Sixth phera. We pray for the health, education, and well-being of our future children.

Seventh phera. We pray for love, friendship, and

eternal companionship.

I watch, silent.

The last time I stood in a temple like this, I had been the one walking around the fire—the one making these promises.

Arun broke every single one.

For years, I hated attending Indian weddings. The vows, the traditions—all of it had felt like a cruel joke. But today... Today, I didn't feel that way.

I feel...healed.

And, as I listen to each vow, Leo pops into my mind.

Would he uphold these things? Yes. Yes, he would.

I know it with a certainty that shakes me. Veera finishes her final phera and locks eyes with me. I know that look—joy, relief, peace. She has found her person. Tears spill down my cheeks, and Saira squeezes my hand in comfort.

Everyone thinks I am crying for Veera.

And I am. But, I am also crying because... I feel healed. Because I don't want to lose Leo. I am realizing—right here, right now—how badly I want to be with him.

I need the support of my girls. Because if I am going to stand up to my parents...

I need strength.

                                   The "I" in Indian

The rest of the day flies by in celebration. Lots of catch-up conversations, tons and tons of pictures, even more sweets. Saira and I get back to our hotel room after dark, ready to shed the heavy outfits and adornments and finally relax. As I slip off the last of my bangles, there is a knock on the door.

We throw it open to find Veera, grinning at us.

And then, all three of us—Aria, Saira, Veera—grab hands, jumping up and down, and scream, "YOU'RE MARRIED!!!"

It is pure joy.

Veera twirls, still buzzing with excitement, her face flushed. Then, she grabs me by the shoulders, pinning me with a look.

"Okay, now that my wedding is over, tell me what the hell is going on with you."

I stiffen. "What?"

Veera rolls her eyes. "Aria, it's written all over your face. Consider this my wedding present. Spill."

I hesitate.

But then... I tell her everything.

I tell her how much I love Leo. How he has been so

patient, so understanding. How he wants a future with me. And how I hurt him because I am keeping him a secret—because I am scared of what my parents will say.

Saira nods. "Dad would probably throw a shit fit."

Veera's eyes blaze. "Aria, you deserve this."

I blink at her.

She grabs my hands, shaking her head in frustration. "You deserve to be happy—to be with someone who understands you, who loves you. To hell with what anyone else thinks! You're the one who has to spend your life with him, not your parents."

I turn to Saira, expecting her to push back.

Instead...she agrees.

"I think you should follow your heart," she says softly. "It's going to be tough. But I'll support you."

I swallow hard, emotion clogging my throat. "But what if Mom and Dad never accept it? What if it confirms that I am a bad Indian girl? What if they..."

I can't say it. What if they disown me?

Veera and Saira look at me.

Veera crosses her arms. "Aria, you just said something ridiculous."

"What?"

"What the hell is a 'good Indian girl.' What does that even mean? How does one 'be' an Indian girl? By following some checklist? By living up to some outdated set of rules?"

I open my mouth, but no words come out.

Veera continues, her voice firm. "Being Indian isn't something you do. It isn't a role you play. It's who you are. I am Indian. Saira is Indian. And you are Indian, Aria. No one gets to take that away from you."

She grabs my hands, squeezing tight. "Indian begins with an 'I.' Now, say it."

I hesitate.

"Say it," Veera presses me.

Saira joins in, her voice soft but insistent. "I am Indian."

I take a shaky breath. "I am Indian."

Veera nods. "Say it louder."

I meet their eyes, my throat tightening.

"I am Indian."

And that can mean whatever I want it to. I...am... Indian.

CHAPTER 30

THIS LANE GOES BOTH WAYS

The road stretches before us, an endless ribbon of asphalt cutting through open fields and occasional patches of trees. The sky is a soft, faded blue, the kind that hints at the first chill of autumn. It is the kind of day that makes you want to roll the windows down and let the wind tangle your hair.

Neither of us has said much since we left the hotel that morning, both lost in our own thoughts. Veera's wedding has stirred something in both of us.

I glance over at Saira. She has one hand on the wheel, the other resting lazily on the armrest. She looks... different. Not in any drastic way, but something about her feels more... open.

Finally, she breaks the silence.

"You know," she says, eyes still on the road, "watching Veera this weekend, it made me think."

I turn to her fully, waiting.

"I think we've spent our whole lives trying to be what Mom and Dad want us to be," she continues. "But maybe it's time we start being who we actually are."

I exhale slowly.

"That's a big statement coming from you."

She let out a small laugh. "I know. But it's true."

For a moment, we sit in silence again, the hum of the car filling the space between us.

"I regret not having an open relationship with them," Saira admits. "I mean, think about it. What if we're missing out on really knowing each other? Like actually knowing each other—not just the version of us that they approve of?"

I frown. "You think they'd even be open to that?"

She sighs. "I don't know. Maybe not. But considering they're older, maybe it has to be us that pushes for the change. Because they're never going to do it themselves."

I swallow, her words settling in my chest.

Then she turns to me with a smirk. "And I think you should be the one to start."

I let out a sharp laugh. "Excuse me? Why me?"

Saira raises a brow, like the answer is obvious. "Because you're older. It's the older sibling tax."

I groan. "That's such bullshit."

She grins. "Maybe. But it's also true. You're the one who always has to go first. You're the one that has to break the status quo."

I look out the window, chewing on my lip. She isn't wrong. The firstborn always takes the brunt of things. I had paved the way for Saira in more ways than one, whether I wanted to or not. And maybe she had never said it out loud before, but I always knew that, after my divorce, she became even more determined to follow the rules.

I glance back at her. "Did you ever resent me for that?"

Saira is quiet for a beat. Then she shakes her head. "No. I think I was scared, though. I saw what you went through, and I thought, 'God, I don't want to feel that.' So, I just... did what they wanted. I kept my head down. I followed the plan."

She hesitates before continuing. "But maybe that's not right, either. Maybe I was too scared of disappointing them. That's why I went to med school."

I blink. "I knew it!" I pause, carefully choosing my words. "Are you saying you don't want to be a doctor?"

Saira lets out a deep breath, staring at the road

ahead. "Not necessarily. I don't know anything else at this point. I do love helping people. And I'm damn good at what I do. So, it worked out. I got lucky."

She shoots me a quick glance. "But I'm the exception. Not the rule."

I understand what she is saying.

She hasn't fought the path set for her, but what if it hadn't been the right one? What if she hadn't loved it? She might have ended up in a career that felt like a cage.

She doesn't want that for me. And she definitely doesn't want me to lose Leo because I am too afraid to stand up to our parents.

Saira's voice softens. "I support you, Aria. I'll stand by you when you talk to them." I swallow hard. The weight of that support means everything.

But something is still unsettled inside me.

I lean forward, my fingers playing with a loose thread on my leggings. "I mean, what even is my culture?"

Saira glances at me, curious. "What do you mean?"

I sigh. "Am I the American girl who drinks vodka sodas, wears bikinis, and eats pasta every week? Or am I the Indian girl who blasts '90s Bollywood every morning while I'm getting ready? Am I the American girl who dates and has boyfriends or the Indian girl who dutifully participates in an arranged marriage? Am I the

   The "I" in Indian

career-driven American woman or the devoted Indian housewife and mother?"

Saira sits back, considering my words.

Then she shrugs. "Why can't you be both?"

That hits me like a ton of bricks.

"Both?"

"Yeah," she says, gesturing with her free hand. "Why do we always feel like we have to pick a side? Like, just because we're Indian-American, we can't embody both identities? You are the girl who drinks vodka sodas and the girl who cries during Bollywood wedding scenes. You can be the girl who dominates her career and learns how to make perfect aloo paratha when she's in the mood. You're not one or the other, Ari. You're both."

I stare at her, letting her words sink in.

"I've always seen it as this constant balancing act. Like I had to prove I am good enough in both worlds. But you're right. I don't have to pick."

"Exactly," Saira says, spearing a piece of chicken from the takeout container on her lap. "Think about it. We get to have the best of both worlds. We get to keep the traditions we love—the food, the music, the family closeness—while also embracing the freedom and opportunities that come with being here. We get to create a life that's uniquely ours."

I lean back in my seat, a sense of clarity washing over me.

"How lucky are we?"

Saira grins. "Pretty damn lucky. We've got two languages, two histories, two sets of holidays. We get to celebrate Navratri and Thanksgiving, watch DDLJ and binge-watch Stranger Things. It's not a burden, Aria. It's a privilege."

I turn my gaze back to the open road ahead of us.

For the first time, being Indian means something new, and I am here for it.

ENTER: A WHOLE NEW ENERGY

Another Sunday lunch at Mom and Dad's. Only this Sunday isn't going to be like the others. Today, I have a mission.

I have spent months hiding what is really going on in my life, avoiding this moment, avoiding this conversation. But after this weekend—after Veera's wedding, after that long drive home with Saira—I know it is time.

I am going to tell my parents about Leo. And I am not leaving until the issue is settled. Or until I walk out of here without a family.

I have to remind myself: My intentions are good. This isn't about defying them. This is about building a better relationship with them—a more open dynamic, one in which we can all be ourselves.

Hopefully, they will see it that way, too. And if not? Then, oh well.

Lunch is as routine as ever.

Mom made red lentils, rice, and okra sabzi, serving us both too much before she even sits down herself. Dad asks his usual questions about work, nodding along as Saira updates him on her residency and I give halfhearted answers about marketing campaigns.

I am waiting. Watching. I need the right moment. Saira, clearly losing patience, kicks me under the table. I shoot her a look, but she just raises her eyebrows. What are you waiting for?

I sigh and put my spoon down. It is now or never.

"So," I start carefully, "Dad, tell me something about yourself from before you got married—from before you were our dad."

He looks up, brows furrowed. "What do you mean?"

"I mean, something about your life before all of this." I gesture around the table. "Did you have other girlfriends? A first love that got away? Any crushes?"

                                    The "I" in Indian

His frown deepens. "Why does that matter?"

"Because it matters to me," I say simply. "I want to know you better."

Mom glances between us, sensing a shift in the conversation.

Dad shakes his head. "Aria, what kind of silly conversation is this? We're eating."

I press on. "Why? Don't you think it makes sense for us to get to know each other better?"

He lets out a short laugh. "Of course, we know each other well enough. Saira is a doctor in the making, and you work in marketing. You're both successful. What else is there to know?"

I scoff. "Really, Dad? You think that's all there is to me?"

Mom stiffens. "Watch your tone when you speak to your father."

I feel the anger rising.

"What is so wrong with talking about things?" I demand. "You're our parents. If we can't talk to you about personal things, then who can we talk to?"

Dad sets his spoon down, his posture tightening. "You and your generation—always talking. Texting, chatting, posting online, constantly sharing. Back in my day, I barely spoke to my parents outside of doing what they asked and showing them my report card."

I clench my fists. "And is that the kind of relationship you want with us?"

Dad's jaw locks.

"Things can change," I press. "Things can evolve. We can build whatever relationship we want. It doesn't have to be the way your parents were with you."

I see the frustration flash across his face. He is shutting down. He is going to walk away. He pushes his chair back. "I'm done eating."

No. Not this time.

Just as he stands up, I throw it out there.

"I am dating an American guy, and I love him."

He freezes. For a moment, there is nothing. Just silence. Then he turns around. His face is blank, unreadable. Saira holds her breath, her hand over her mouth. Mom's eyes widen. She turns sharply to Saira.

"Did you know about this?" Her voice is laced with shock, accusation. "You knew she is dating this guy?"

Saira hesitates for only a second before nodding. "Yes." Mom's face darkens. "Saira..."

Saira straightens. "I've met him, Mom. He's a really nice man, and I think if you just meet him, you'd..."

But Mom cuts her off, "Enough!" The single word shuts down the conversation.

Saira flinches slightly but stays quiet.

And then Mom turns back to me, voice tight. "Aria,

what do you mean you love him? How? You know that
can't work."

I let out a dry laugh. "And why not?"

Mom's lips press together. "Because he is American.
We have completely different cultures and values."

There it is.

I shake my head. "What values are you talking
about? He has wonderful values. He is committed to me.
He will never hurt me."

I turn to Dad, voice shaking. "I married an Indian
man. What values did he have? He didn't think twice
before abandoning me, before breaking his promises.
What kind of 'value' is that?"

Dad still doesn't say anything.

Mom is horrified. "Aria, what will people say?"

I let out an exhausted laugh. "Seriously, Mom?
Aren't we tired of this? 'What will people say?' They
already say plenty. I'm already divorced, remember?
This'll just be one more thing that makes me 'damaged.'
"

I take a deep breath, "We think you've been
wonderful parents." My voice softens. Mom and Dad
both look at me, slightly thrown off. "You have provided
everything for us. We never went without. But we have
also been good kids."

I gesture toward Saira. "Look at Saira. She's a

freaking doctor! And I turned out to be a good person. We are not so bad, are we?"

They don't respond. I press on.

"So, what if we don't live up to some weird standard of what an Indian girl is 'supposed' to be? We did grow up here after all. And you brought us here for a better life, anyway. Aren't we still lovable? Don't you still love us?"

The silence stretches out. Too long. Way too long.

I feel something crack inside me.

I push back my chair and stand up.

Fine.

If they need time to process this, I am done waiting.

I stand up sharply, put my chin up, square my shoulders, turn toward the door, and start marching, heart pounding. I am not going to spend my entire life trying to please my parents. If anyone truly loves me, they will accept me for who I am.

I reach for the handle...

"Aria, wait."

My father's voice.

I freeze.

Slowly, I turn around.

He meets my eyes, his own face still unreadable.

And then...

"When can we meet him?"

CHAPTER 32

BOLLYWOOD SET THE BAR

The next night, my heart is still thudding in my chest from last night's conversation with my parents. I had confronted them. I finally stood up for myself, for my happiness, for Leo. And while it had been the most difficult conversation of my life, it had also brought me an unexpected gift—my father's willingness to meet Leo. That single act gave me a newfound optimism— one that I had not dared to feel before. Anxiety had transformed miraculously into an excitement about my future with Leo.

I picked up my phone and texted Leo.

Come over. I have something I want to share with you.

He responded almost instantly.

Be there in 30.

As I wait, I set up the living room. I pull out the cozy blankets, dim the lights, and pop a bag of popcorn. Tonight, I am going to break it to Leo that we can, in fact, have a future together. I want to do it in a way that will help him to better understand my culture and what he's getting himself into. If I am being honest, I always wanted to share this piece of myself, a piece I had long feared I would have to let go of if I chose to be with someone outside my culture.

When Leo arrives, I greet him with a warm smile and a quick kiss before leading him to the couch. "We're watching an Indian movie tonight," I announce, handing him a bowl of popcorn.

"Oh?" He plops down beside me. "What are we watching?"

I grab the remote and pull up Dilwale Dulhania Le Jayenge. "It's one of the most popular Bollywood films of all time. It's been playing in theaters for like 20 years straight."

Leo's brows shoot up. "Twenty years? That's insane."

"It's a classic," I say, curling my legs underneath me. "And it's important to me. I want to see how you experience it."

He gives me a curious look but nods. "Alright, let's do it."

As the movie starts, I steal glances at Leo, waiting for his reactions.

The story follows Simran, a young woman from a strict Indian family, who has been promised since childhood to someone in an arranged marriage. But, before she resigns herself to that fate, she convinces her father to let her take a month-long trip across Europe with her friends. It is on this trip that she meets Raj— carefree, mischievous, and completely wrong for her in every way that matters. At first, they clash. Simran finds him arrogant, immature, and too flirtatious for her taste. But, over time, her irritation turns into something else. Through chance encounters, stolen glances, and unexpected moments of kindness, they fall in love.

Simran knows that love alone isn't enough. She has made a promise to her father, and she intends to honor it. She returns home to India, ready to marry a man she barely knows, prepared to put her feelings for Raj aside. But Raj isn't willing to let her go so easily. He makes a bold choice. Disguising himself as a wedding guest, he is on a mission to win her family over. The wedding festivities carry on for a week, during which time everyone stays in the same house and spends all day and night together. He shows kindness to her mother and respect to her father. He finds camaraderie with her sibling. Slowly, painstakingly, he makes himself a crucial part of the wedding, proving that he is someone worthy of their love and trust.

Then comes the moment of truth. When Simran's father discovers the truth about their relationship, his rage is swift and unforgiving. Raj is cast out. Simran is told she will marry as planned. Love is dismissed as foolish fantasy. It is then that Simran fights for what she wants. She pleads with her father to let her choose her own happiness. When she is unsuccessful, she desperately asks Raj to elope. But, Raj refuses. He tells her he will only marry her with her father's blessing.

Leo is riveted. He barely moves as the climax unfolds on the train platform. Simran's desperate cries, her father's final moment of surrender, moved by Raj's integrity and respect for their traditions. He released his daughter's hand and lets her run to Raj. I feel the familiar swell of emotions that come every time I watch the movie. Love has won. Family has softened. Tradition has made room for happiness.

As the credits roll, I turn to Leo. "That's what I wanted you to see," I say softly. "Indian fathers... They can be tough, but, at the end of it all, they love their daughters. And sometimes, even when it takes everything in them, they bend for their happiness."

   The "I" in Indian

Leo looks at me for a long moment before reaching for my hand. "Would your dad bend for you?"

I nod, squeezing his fingers. "He wants to meet you."

A slow smile spreads across Leo's face, his eyes filled with something between relief and joy. He lifts our joined hands to his lips and kisses the back of mine. "Time to turn my inner Raj on."

I exhale, the last remnants of fear melting away. From childhood, Bollywood movies have shaped my ideas of love. I have grown up watching grand, sweeping romances in which love always triumphs, obstacles are overcome, and happy endings are inevitable. For a long time, I wasn't sure if I would get my own happy ending. My failed marriage left me jaded, doubtful that I would ever experience the kind of love I had spent my life watching unfold on screen.

But now, with Leo, I finally feel it. I am in my own Bollywood love story. Not perfect, not scripted—but real. And for the first time, I believe that this time, love will win.

CHAPTER 33
THE HARBOR TEST

The hum of Bollywood music playing softly in the car sets the stage for what could either be a lovely evening or a complete disaster.

I smooth down my shirt one last time, take a deep breath, and adjust the bouquet of flowers in my lap. Beside me, Aria grips the steering wheel, her knuckles a little too tight. I can tell she is nervous, and, frankly, so am I.

In the back seat, Saira stretches her legs out casually, balancing a thermos of chai in one hand like she has zero concerns about how tonight will go.

"So," she says, her voice dripping with mock seriousness, "are you two ready to face the parental firing squad?"

I turn around to face her, half-smiling, half-terrified. "I think I'm ready. But should I be more worried than I already am?"

"Oh, definitely," Saira deadpanned. "My dad can smell fear. And my mom? She can see right through you. If you're lying about liking her samosas, she'll know."

I let out a nervous laugh, shifting in my seat.

"Saira!" Aria hisses, glaring at her in the rearview mirror. "You're not helping."

Saira just grins, completely unbothered. "Relax, Ari. Leo's got this. I mean, he's already met me, and I'm obviously the toughest critic in the family."

I chuckle despite myself. "That's true. If I survived you, I think I might have a shot with your parents."

"Exactly," she says, leaning back smugly.

I appreciate that she is making light of the situation, but it doesn't erase the weight pressing on my chest.

This isn't just a dinner. This is **the** dinner. The one where I am going to prove to Aria's parents that I am not some temporary fling, that I am not a stranger to be feared. That I can belong in their world, just as much as I belong in Aria's.

When we pull up to her parents' house, my heart rate picks up. The three of us climb out of the car.

Saira, ever the troublemaker, grabs the flowers from my hand and whispers, "Good luck, Romeo." Then she saunters off toward the door like she owns the place.

I take a deep breath. No turning back now. "You ready?"

    The "I" in Indian

Aria asks.

I adjust my collar and give her a reassuring smile, even though my stomach is doing flips. "As ready as I'll ever be. And I even practiced how to say 'Namaste' correctly."

That earns a small laugh, easing the tension just a little.

"They speak English" she says, squeezing my hand. "You'll be fine."

I am not so sure about that.

When the door opens, Aria's mom stands there, small but regal. Aria looks so much like her mother. The same big eyes, bright smile, and olive skin. Her pale sari was perfectly pinned, her expression unreadable as her gaze moves over the three of us—lingering a little longer on me.

I don't hesitate. I press my palms together and say, "Namaste."

Her eyebrows lift slightly, but she nods in approval. "Namaste. Please, come in."

The house smells like masala and fresh roti, and I feel my nerves tangle even tighter as I step inside. In the living room, Aria's dad is seated, reading the newspaper.

He looks up, his glasses slipping slightly down his nose. His eyes land on me, scanning me for just a moment before standing up to greet me.

This is the moment.

I swallow. Aria speaks first.

"Leo, these are my parents, Shama and Vishal," she says,

her voice steady despite the tension in the air. "Ma, Papa, this is Leo, my boyfriend."

The word hangs between us, foreign in this house.

I braced myself. Before her parents can react, Saira swoops in.

"Just to be clear, Papa," Sairi says, plopping onto the couch like she has been waiting for this all day. " 'Boyfriend' means he's not here to propose or anything. Yet."

"Saira!" Aria snaps at her sister, turning bright red. Saira is enjoying this too much.

"What?" she says innocently, batting her lashes. "I'm just setting expectations."

I want to laugh, but I also want to die.

Aria's dad slowly folds his newspaper, his gaze shifting from Saira to Aria and then to me.

"Boyfriend, huh?"

Here it comes.

"Yes, Papa," Aria says firmly. "Leo and I are adults. We're figuring things out together. He's important to me."

I see her mom purse her lips slightly before taking the flowers from Saira and disappearing into the kitchen. Maybe I should step in and say something?

"Boyfriend—only for now, though," I say, extending my hand to shake his. Hoping my openness about my intention would set the right tone.

Her dad, after one last long look at me, extends his hand.

　　　　　　　　　The "I" in Indian

"Welcome," he says gruffly.

I could have sagged with relief.

"Thank you, sir," I say, shaking his hand firmly.

As the evening progresses, the air between us all feels lighter than I had expected. There is no tension or unspoken disapproval, no judgment lingering over Aria's past. She has confronted her demons, and her parents no longer view her divorce as a stain on her life. Instead, they see her happiness, her authenticity, and they embrace it.

Dinner is a feast of flavors, an explosion of spices that dance on my tongue. I eat enthusiastically, savoring every bite of the homemade dishes Aria's mother has lovingly prepared. The warmth of the fresh roti. The depth of the lentils. The rich, buttery paneer. It is all incredible. I clear my plate twice, which seems to please Aria's mom immensely.

At one point, as we sip chai, Aria's dad turns to me. "So, Leo, has Aria shown you any Bollywood movies?"

I grin. "Actually, we just watched Dilwale Dulhania Le Jayenge. It was amazing."

Her mom's eyebrows raise slightly. "Oh?"

"I love how Raj won over Simran's family instead of just running away with her," I say. "It moved me because I think it's important to respect the family and values of your partner."

Aria's dad gives a thoughtful nod. "That is... a good answer."

Aria beams at me, and, for the first time that evening, I felt like I could fit right in here.

As we leave, Aria's mom stands at the door, this time with a small smile. "It was nice meeting you, Leo." She gives Aria a shy look, which feels loaded with approval.

"Thank you for having me," I reply. "And for the delicious food. I'd love to come back and try new dishes next time."

That earns me a small laugh from Aria's dad. "Already getting comfortable, huh?"

I smile as we wave goodbye.

As the doors to the car close, Aria sags her shoulders and lets out a huge sigh of relief. Saira reaches around from the back of the car and pats me on the shoulder. "Well done, my friend." Aria reaches over and squeezes my hand, fighting back happy tears as we drive off.

Nailed it.

<h1 style="text-align:center">EPILOGUE</h1>

LEADING LADY

The summer sun beams through the trees as I stand at home base, my heart racing and laughter bubbling from my chest. Leo's nieces and nephews dart around the makeshift field, their tiny sneakers kicking up little clouds of dust as they holler instructions to one another. His mom, Maria, stands in the outfield, waving her glove in mock intimidation. And then there is Leo, standing on the pitcher's mound with that easy, confident grin that makes my heart flutter every single time.

"Alright, Aria," he calls out, gripping the tennis ball in his hand like a prized artifact. "Are you ready for this?"

I adjust my grip on the bat, planting my feet firmly. "Bring it on, Roselli!"

The ball hurtles toward me—not too fast, but not too slow, either—and I swing with all my might. The satisfying thwack of the ball meeting the broomstick sends a cheer through the yard as the ball sails past Leo and into Maria's section of the field.

"Run, Aria, run!" shouts Leo's dad, laughing as he waves me toward first base.

I take off, my feet pounding as Leo pretends to chase me down, dramatically diving for the ball in a show of mock defeat. By the time I reach third base, I am breathless and beaming.

This is our Sunday. Stickball games with Leo's family has become a cherished afternoon tradition over the past year. It is chaotic and messy and loud, but it is also filled with so much love. And for me, it is the perfect balance of everything I have been searching for. Sunday lunches with my parents, Sunday afternoon in the sun with his. Today, my parents came, too. To my surprise, my dad yells often from the sideline and enjoys himself.

As I jog toward home plate, catching my breath, I notice Leo walking toward me. His expression has softened, and there is something in his eyes—something more than love, something deeper, steadier.

"Hold up, Aria," he says, stopping me in my tracks.

I raise an eyebrow, glancing around the yard. The game has stopped. Everyone is watching. My parents,

   The "I" in Indian

standing near the sidelines with cautious but amused expressions. Saira is there, too, grinning knowingly, her arms crossed as if she already knows what is coming.

"What's going on?" I ask, suddenly aware of the way my heart is thundering in my chest.

Leo doesn't answer right away. Instead, he reaches into his pocket, pulling out a small velvet box. My breath catches.

"Oh, my God," I whisper, my hand instinctively covering my mouth.

Leo gives a glance over to my father, an exchange I don't miss. My dad gives the nod of approval. Clearly, they've talked about this. Leo drops to one knee, holding the box up to reveal the most beautiful solitaire ring I have ever seen. The sunlight catches the diamond, making the princess cut sparkle like it holds its own little piece of the sky.

"Aria Kapoor," he begins, his voice steady and warm, "I knew from the moment I saw you that you are someone special. But what I didn't know was just how much you would change my life. You have taught me about love, resilience, and what it means to truly share a life with someone. I don't just love you; I admire you. And I can't imagine a future without you in it."

Tears fill my eyes as he continues.

"I want to spend the rest of my life with you. I want

to keep watching Bollywood movies with you, cooking Indian food together, and playing stickball with our families. I want to build a life that's as dynamic and beautiful as you are. So, what do you say? Will you marry me?"

For a moment, all I can do is nod, tears streaming down my cheeks as the world around us erupts into cheers and applause.

"Yes," I finally manage to say, my voice trembling with emotion. "Yes, Leo Roselli, I will marry you."

He slides the ring onto my finger. Before I can process anything else, he is on his feet, wrapping me in the kind of hug that makes everything else fade away.

As we stand there, surrounded by both of our families—by the love and chaos and laughter that now defines our lives, I realize something profound.

This moment isn't just about saying yes to Leo. It is about saying yes to myself—to my journey and to the dynamic, beautiful life we are creating together.

As Leo kisses me in the middle of that makeshift baseball field, a memory from years ago surfaces—of me as a little girl, sitting cross-legged in front of the TV, watching my favorite Bollywood movies. I used to believe in the kind of love those films promised— unconditional, undying, forever kind.

At some point, life made me skeptical of that love.

It felt too cinematic, too unattainable. But here is Leo, proving me wrong with every moment, every touch, every word. He is my Bollywood hero—the one who didn't just rescue me but walked beside me as I rescued myself.

In him, I had found the kind of love I once thought only existed on screen. Unwavering. Patient. Deeply kind. The kind of love that didn't ask me to shrink but encouraged me to grow. The kind of love that encouraged me to be me, all of me.

The kind of love that feels like home.

This isn't just the end of one chapter or the beginning of another. This is the story I had been waiting for all along—the one in which I get to be the heroine of my own life with someone by my side who believes in me just as much as I believe in myself.

And as I look at Leo, my heart swelling with gratitude and love, I know this isn't just the beginning of something extraordinary. It is the life I was always meant to live.

The End

Coming Soon from Bhavna Bhatia Roszel:

NO PERMISSION NEEDED

CHAPTER 1
NAMASTE... LET'S RAGE

The shuttle isn't even here yet, and I'm already sweating.

The California sun is doing its thing—bright, blazing, and completely unforgiving. But, honestly, I don't care. I'm too excited to care. This is it. The mother of all music festivals. After weeks of plotting, pestering, and borderline manipulation, I've finally convinced both Aria and Anjali to come to Coachella with me. A feat that deserves some kind of award.

I lean against a palm tree near the curb, letting the sliver of shadow cool one shoulder. My phone buzzes with a text, but I ignore it. I'm focused on the moment—the anticipation buzzing in my chest, the promise of pounding bass and flashing lights just hours away.

This is my kind of therapy. Loud music, massive crowds, enough stimulation to drown out even the noisiest corners of my mind. I don't want to sip wine and decompress. I want to lose myself in a crowd so big that I forget I exist.

Aria, of course, prefers the wine-and-book combo. Her idea of relaxation includes candles and silence. But, she recently closed on a beautiful townhome. After the Krishastation that fucker put her through, she deserves to celebrate. Me? I like to be shoved shoulder-to-shoulder with strangers while a DJ tries to out-bass my trauma.

Getting her to agree took some serious emotional warfare.

"I swear to God, Veera," she groaned last week during our final phone call, "if you bring up this festival one more time, I'm blocking your number. I'm still decorating the new place. My boss wants five impossible things done by Tuesday."

"Which is exactly why you need this," I told her. "You don't need a break to reset. You don't need a nap. You need chaos. My kind of chaos."

She finally cracked, mostly out of exhaustion. "Fine," she said.

Anjali was tougher. She just opened her first yoga studio—a lifelong dream, finally realized—and was riding high on mantras, tea blends, and sustainable

　　　　　　　　No Permission Needed

incense. Her vibe is...well, very not Coachella.

So, I did what any supportive best friend would do: I lied.

"Think of it as an energetic convergence," I told her over FaceTime. "A sacred communal space for celebration. Thousands of people aligning their vibrations under the stars. It's practically a sound bath with glitter."

She narrowed her eyes. "You're full of crap."

"Sure. But are you coming?"

She sighed. "Only because you said 'sacred convergence' with a straight face."

So here I am, standing outside my apartment building in downtown LA, waiting for my girls to emerge. The sliding glass doors are spotless as ever, reflecting a vision of me that looks way too hype for 9:00 am.

My 10th floor loft is all mine—high ceilings, huge windows, zero roommates. And sure, I brag about the independence, but truth is? It's lonely sometimes. Neither Aria nor Anjali live anywhere close, and the dating pool? I'd rather dive into literal fire.

The doors slide open, and just like that, they're here.

Denim booty shorts? Check.

Neon green bandos and black mesh throws? Check.

Sunglasses, tiny backpacks, and general hot-girl

energy? Absolutely.

They walk out like a runway duo, and I feel my heart expand just looking at them. Aria, with her high ponytail and deeply skeptical expression. It's been three years since Arun left, and here she is, stunning. Anjali is glowing like she just walked off the set of a coconut water commercial.

"My thighs are already chafing," Aria grumbles as they reach me. "Why do I let you talk me into these things?"

"Because you love me," I grin, pulling her into a hug.

"And because I threatened to manifest a blockage in your root chakra if you said no," Anjali adds, arms wide as she gathers us both in.

"This is going to be magical," she beams.

"I'm counting on it," I say. "I need to not think for, like, three days straight."

We pile into the shuttle, which smells like patchouli, sunscreen, and excitement—aka my favorite blend. I settle into my seat by the window and let my head fall back. The sun is golden through the windshield, the kind of light that makes everything feel cinematic.

I don't think about work. I don't think about my parents. I don't think about the string of dead-end situationships I've dragged myself through just to pass

No Permission Needed

the time.

Maybe I'm jaded for life. Maybe I'll be alone forever. But that's not something I'm letting myself think about right now.

Right now, there's music ahead. A sea of strangers. A pulse I can lose myself in.

And for once, that's enough.

CHAPTER 2

LOST MY FRIENDS (ON PURPOSE)

I've been here for hours, and I've officially "lost" my friends. The sun is starting to set, and I'm not in the mood to spend another night nodding along while a bunch of almost-30 guys in neon tanks ogle girls in outfits that look like they lost a bet with a glitter bomb.

And the conversations? Brutal. Every time I try to have a meaningful exchange—something, anything—it gets hijacked by TikTok trends or someone's follower count.

"I went viral for this dance last week."

"My Reels engagement has been so off since the algorithm changed."

"Should I get lip filler or just overline forever?"

My brain is melting.

These aren't conversations. They're captions.

I move through the crowd alone, drink in hand, trying not to get elbowed by someone filming their 15th Instagram Story of the hour. It's exhausting. And fake. And maybe I'm just bitter, but none of it feels real. Not like the world I work in.

As a program director for a global health nonprofit, I spend most of my days coordinating medical brigades to underserved communities—places where people are dying for antibiotics, not Wi-Fi. Places where there's no running water, no toilets, no emergency rooms. Where "influencer culture" couldn't be more meaningless.

So, yeah, maybe I'm not in the mood to hear about some girl's anxiety over whether her lavender nails match her vibe.

Or maybe it's something else.

Maybe it's because Holi just passed. And that weekend used to mean something.

Back home in India, my family used to go all out. Our farmhouse would be packed with relatives, music, colors flying through the air, the smell of fresh jalebis and spicy chaat wafting from the kitchen. My sister and I would run barefoot through the lawn, staining each other pink and blue until we were unrecognizable. It's been 10 years since I celebrated with them.

So yeah, I'm a little off tonight.

The DJ's set is incredible, though—a slow build into a

thunderous drop that vibrates straight through the ground. I close my eyes for a second, letting the rhythm numb everything sharp inside of me.

And then...A jolt.

Someone slams into my side, almost toppling over, and knocking my beer right out of my hand. I instinctively reach out and catch her by the arm.

"Whoa...easy..." I start, but she's already snapping upright.

Shiny black curls fall across her face before she pushes them back, revealing full lips, sharp eyes, and absolutely no trace of apology.

"Oops," she says, flatly, already turning away.

No "sorry." No "thanks." Just that one snarky little word. And...she's gone. This is exactly what I'm talking about.

Well, not gone. She's 5 feet in front of me, already dancing like nothing happened.

Her friends are with her, clearly part of some coordinated look. One of them—tall, glowy, the kind of woman who probably does yoga on cliffs—turns back and mouths, "Sorry."

I give her a nod, but I'm still staring at her. The rude one. The wild one.

She's dancing with abandon—shuffling, twirling, flipping her hair and banging her head to the beat like it's the only thing that matters. There's something so unapologetic about it. So free.

And, damn, if it isn't sexy as hell.

I should look away. I should find my friends. I should go back to pretending I'm just here for the music. But instead, I plant my feet and relax into my stance. I've decided. Tonight, this—she—is my view.

CHAPTER 3

BEARDS, B.S., AND BAD IDEAS

I know I'm drunk because I'm staring at a stranger's beard like it's art.

But damn, it's a really good beard. Perfectly trimmed, thick. Not the try-hard kind that looks like it came with a kit, but the kind that just happens to exist naturally on really lucky men.

And he's tall. Like "let me climb you like a tree" tall. His hair is thick, his lashes are unfairly long. And, when the stage lights hit just right, his cheekbones do this ridiculous thing that should be illegal in public spaces.

Of course, I had to bump into him.

I didn't even apologize. Just a lazy "oops," like a brat. To be fair, I was mid-sprint to the front of the stage because my actual song came on, and, well, priorities are priorities. But now?

Now, I can feel him watching me.

I try to lose myself in the music, to let the beat swallow the awkwardness, but it's impossible to ignore the burn of his gaze. I look back. He's definitely looking. I look away. Then look back again. Still looking.

God, stop staring, Veera. But he's not creepy about it. More curious. Intrigued.

Okay, fine. Let's just...clear the air. The DJ is being changed right now anyway, so there's a pause in the music. I need something to do. I march back toward him, tipsy and entirely too confident.

"I know I spilled your beer," I shout. "Take it as a lesson for what happens when you get in my way. But, you don't have to keep giving me the death glare."

His eyes crinkle slightly. He's smiling now—ugh. And his teeth? White. Perfect. Kryptonite. I need to leave.

"That's not why I was staring at you," he says smoothly.

Is he...flirting?

He says it like a statement, not a question. Like he's used to being bold and getting away with it. Ballsy. I narrow my eyes at him, just as I catch the faintest trace of something in his voice.

    No Permission Needed

Wait. Is that...an accent?

"Are you—Indian?" I ask, leaning in slightly.

He raises an eyebrow. "Yes. You picked up on that?"

"I've got the radar," I say flatly. "How long have you been here?"

"A decade."

"Same," I say, carefully. I don't offer more. I don't owe him my life story just because his jawline is stupidly symmetrical.

"Where in India?" I ask.

"Delhi."

"Same." My answer is clipped, but it hangs in the air between us, almost too neat to be real.

I give him a once-over. From the neck up? Devastating. From the neck down? Khaki shorts. A blue polo. Tucked in.

"You do realize this is a music festival, right?" I say, gesturing at his outfit. "Not your little cousin's graduation party."

He laughs, a low, warm sound that curls somewhere in my chest.

"So, Mr. Indian Man," I go on, smirking, "what do you do for a living? Let me guess... doctor? Engineer? Own a 7-Eleven? Drive a cab? Or are you saving the world one IT problem at a time?"

He snorts. Doesn't even flinch. That earns him

a few points. "Something like that," he says. "I work for a nonprofit. I help coordinate medical missions in underserved countries."

Oh.

My mouth opens slightly, but I shut it quickly. The last thing I need is to be impressed. A guy who cares about kids and saving the world? Absolutely not. That is enemy #1. A walking trap. A honey-glazed heartbreak waiting to happen.

Don't fall for the beard, Veera. Don't fall for the teeth. Don't fall for the soul.

I snap myself out of it and look around. Where are my girls?

I spot Aria first—yawning, arms crossed, silently motioning toward the camp area. Anjali's rubbing her feet and nodding along like she just received a divine message.

Time to go.

"Well," I say abruptly, "looks like my friends are done for the night. Gotta walk them back to our tent."

I turn without ceremony. No parting smile. No flirtatious linger. Done and done.

But then I hear him call out behind me.

"Can I come with you?"

I stop dead. Turn slowly. "Why the fuck would you come with me?"

He grins. Innocent. Too innocent.

"You owe me a drink."

Damn it. I do owe him a drink. Technically. And it's just a walk, right?

I glance at his stupidly hopeful face, his stupidly white teeth, and his even stupider boyish charm.

"Fine," I sigh. "But you're not getting any foot rubs if you get tired."

He jogs to catch up.

I'm already regretting this.

Sort of.

Scan to Order
Additional Books

Stay in the Loop!

Scan to learn more about events, including author signings, readings, and future releases